On the Ribble riverside, leaving Preston (Stage 22)

WALKING THE KING CHARLES III ENGLAND COAST PATH: NORTH WEST – LANCASHIRE & MERSEYSIDE

This guidebook describes the Lancashire and Merseyside section of the 590km (367 mile) King Charles III England Coast Path in the north west. It covers the National Trail from Arnside to Chester along the Lancashire and Merseyside coastline. This convenient and compact booklet shows the route, providing all the mapping you need to walk the trail in either direction.

Contents and using this guide
This booklet of Ordnance Survey 1:25,000 Explorer® maps has been designed for convenient use on the trail and includes:
- a key to map pages (page 2) showing where to find the maps for each stage.
- the full and up-to-date line of the National Trail designed for use northbound or southbound.
- an extract from the OS Explorer map legend (pages 82–85).

The companion guidebook – *Walking the King Charles III England Coast Path: North West* – describes the full route in both directions with lots of other practical and historical information.

© Cicerone Press 2025
First edition 2025
ISBN: 978 1 78631 041 5
Photos © Ange Harker 2025
© Crown copyright and database rights 2025 OS AC0000810376
Printed in Singapore by KHL Printing on responsibly sourced paper.
Cicerone's EU representative for GPSR compliance is Easy Access System Europe, Mustamäe tee 50, 10621 Tallinn, Estonia. Email gpsr.requests@easproject.com.

THE KING CHARLES III ENGLAND COAST PATH: NORTH WEST

Stage 16	Arnside to Hest Bank	7
Stage 17	Hest Bank to Overton	13
Stage 18	Overton to Conder Green	18
Stage 19	Conder Green to Knott End	19
Stage 20	Fleetwood to Lytham	26
Stage 21	Lytham to Preston	39
Stage 22	Preston to Tarleton	45
Stage 23	Tarleton to Crossens	47
Stage 24	Crossens to Formby	51
Stage 25	Formby to Seaforth	56
Stage 26	Seaforth to New Brighton	60
Stage 27	New Brighton to Parkgate	62
Stage 28	Parkgate to Chester	73

Stages 1–15 . . . . Cumbria booklet

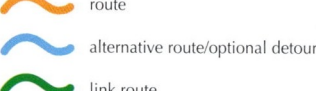

Route symbols on OS map extracts

- route
- alternative route/optional detour
- link route
- (SF) start/finish point
- (SF) alternative start/finish point
- ˙˙˙˙˙ ferry route

for OS legend see printed OS maps

SCALE: 1:25,000

0 kilometres 0.5 1
0 miles 0.5

GPX files
for all routes can be downloaded free at
www.cicerone.co.uk/1041/GPX

On the marsh wall approaching Parkgate (Stage 27)

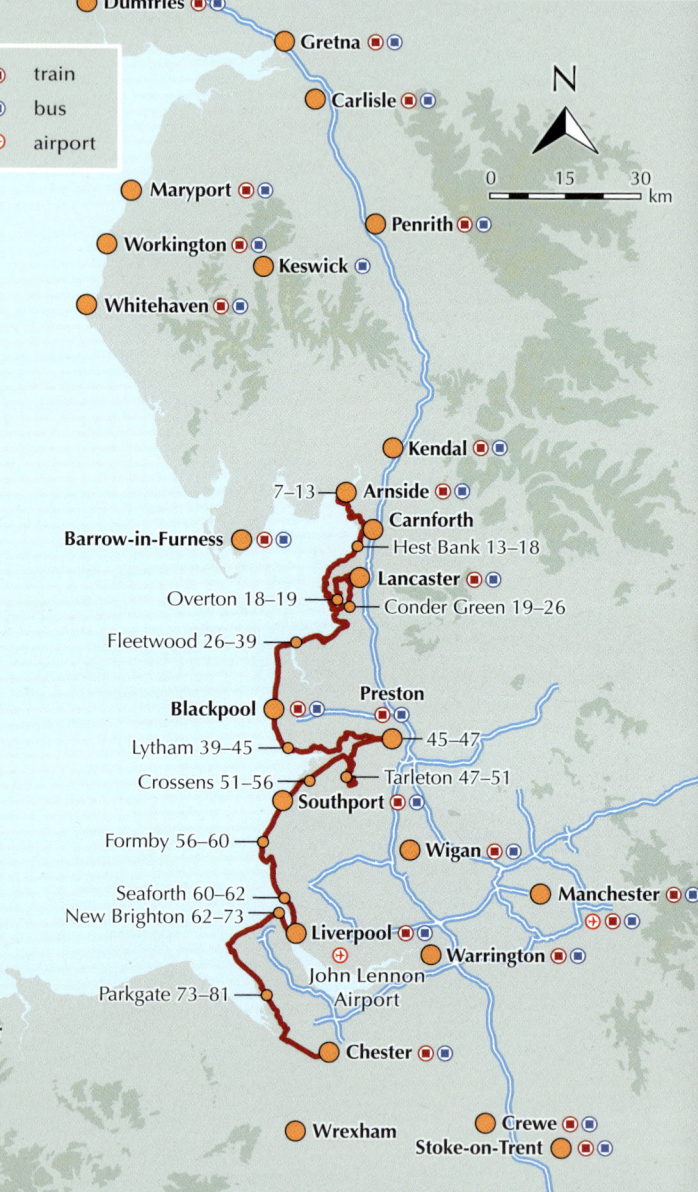

The iconic Blackpool Tower oversees the town's central pier, beach and multi-level prom, with plenty of attractions to keep you entertained (Stage 20)

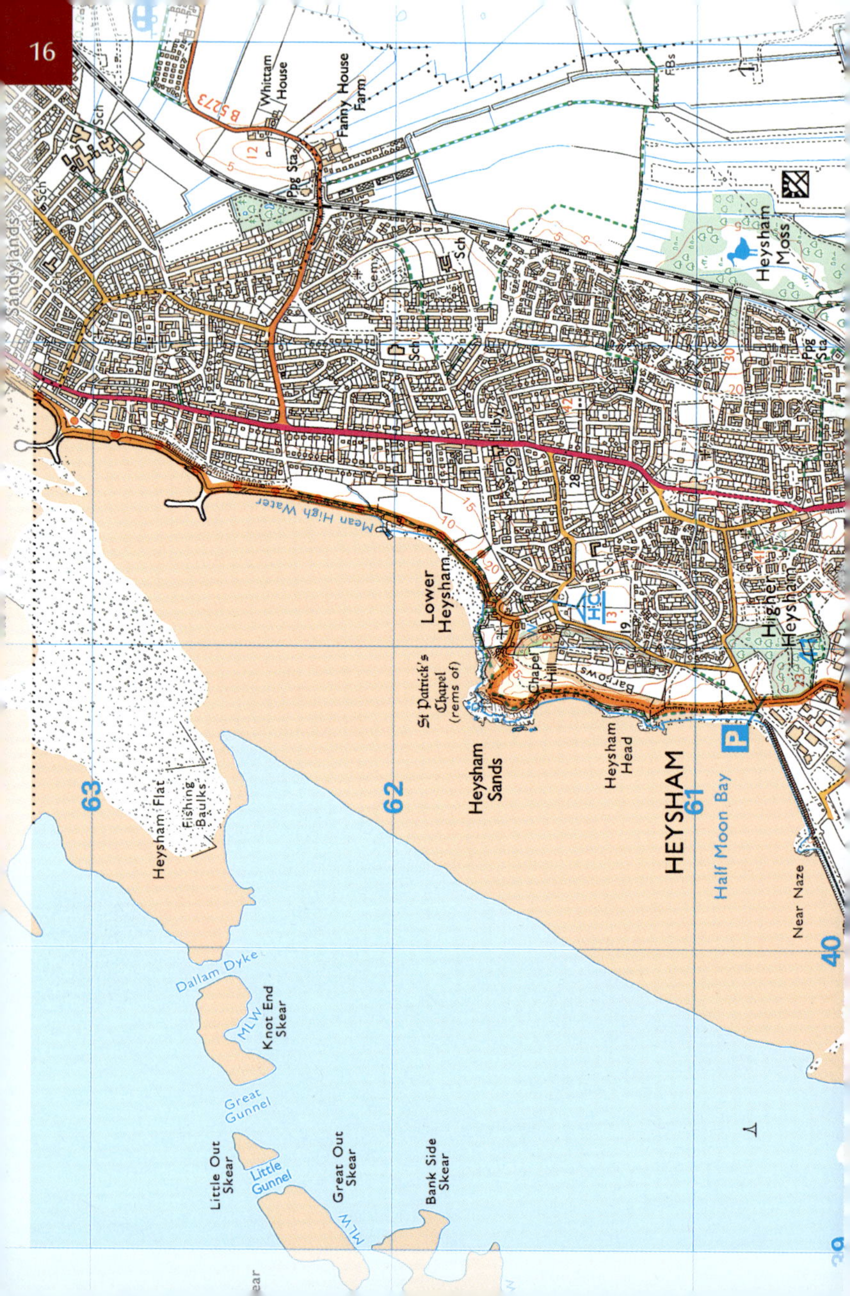

Sandylands
Sch
Whittam House
Fanny House Farm
B5273
Ppg Sta
Cemy
Sch
FBs
Heysham Moss
Ppg Sta
Lby
PO
Mean High Water
Lower Heysham
St Patrick's Chapel (rems of)
Chapel Hill
Barrows
HC
Higher Heysham
Heysham Sands
Heysham Head
HEYSHAM
Half Moon Bay
Near Naze
Heysham Flat
Fishing Baulks
Dallam Dyke
MLW
Knot End Skear
Great Gunnel
Little Out Skear
Little Gunnel
Great Out Skear
Bank Side Skear
63
62
61
40

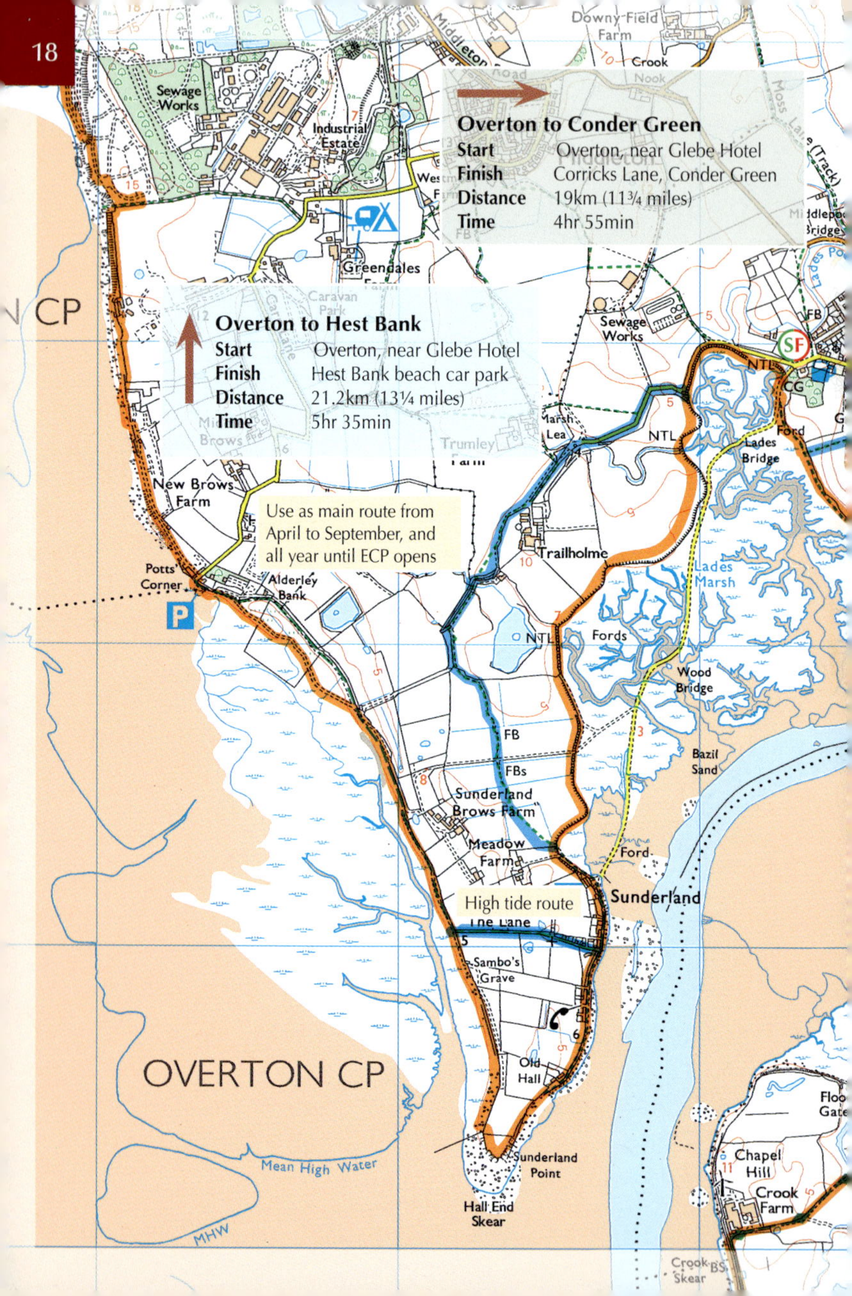

Overton to Conder Green
Start Overton, near Glebe Hotel
Finish Corricks Lane, Conder Green
Distance 19km (11¾ miles)
Time 4hr 55min
Overton to Hest Bank
Start Overton, near Glebe Hotel
Finish Hest Bank beach car park
Distance 21.2km (13¼ miles)
Time 5hr 35min
Use as main route from April to September, and all year until ECP opens
High tide route
Sewage Works
Industrial Estate
Downy Field Farm
Crook Nook
Middleton Road
Moss Lane (Track)
Middlepool Bridge
Greendales Farm
Caravan Park
Sewage Works
Marsh Lea
Trumley Farm
New Brows Farm
Potts' Corner
Alderley Bank
Trailholme
NTL
Lades Bridge
Lades Marsh
Fords
Wood Bridge
Bazil Sand
FB
FBs
Sunderland Brows Farm
Meadow Farm
Ford
Sunderland
The Lane
Sambo's Grave
Old Hall
Sunderland Point
Hall End Skear
OVERTON CP
Mean High Water
MHW
Chapel Hill
Crook Farm
Flood Gate
Crook BS Skear
SF
CG

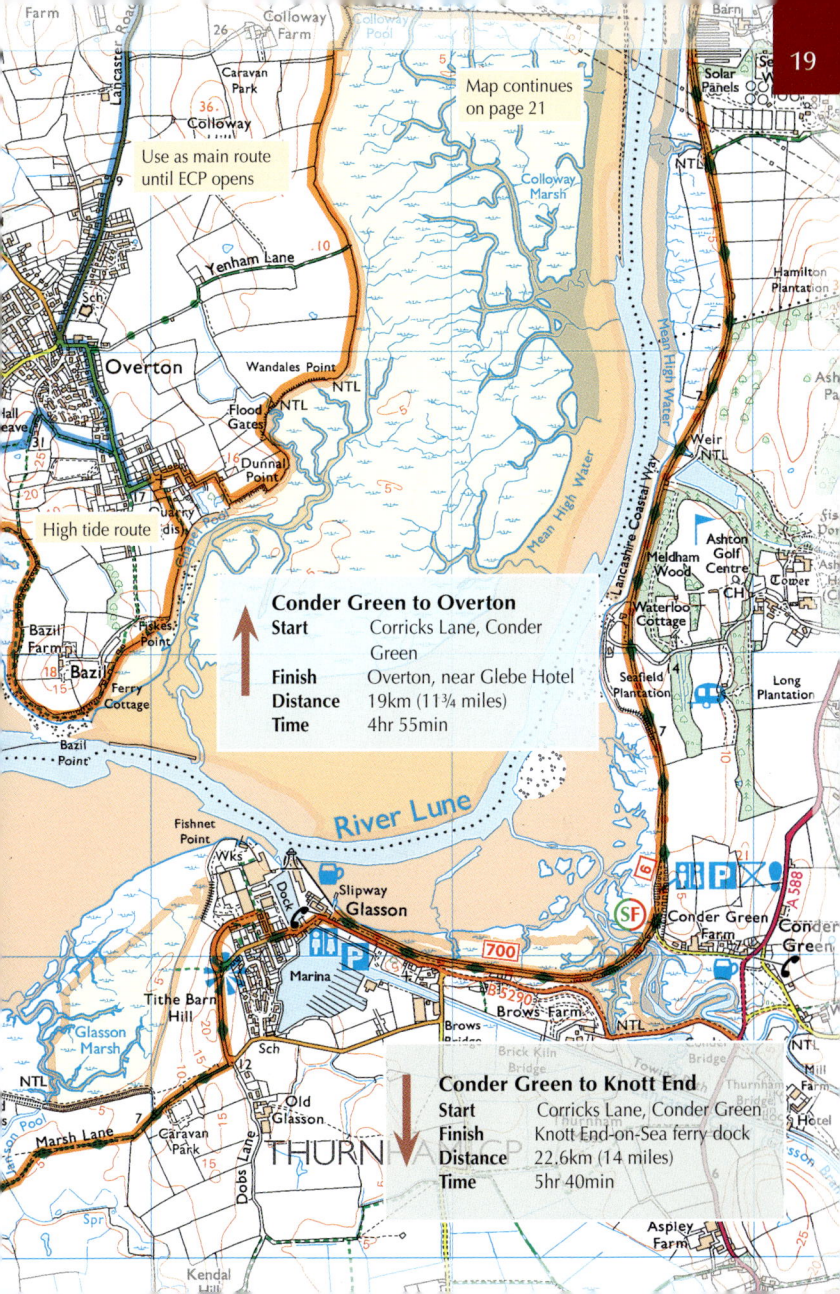

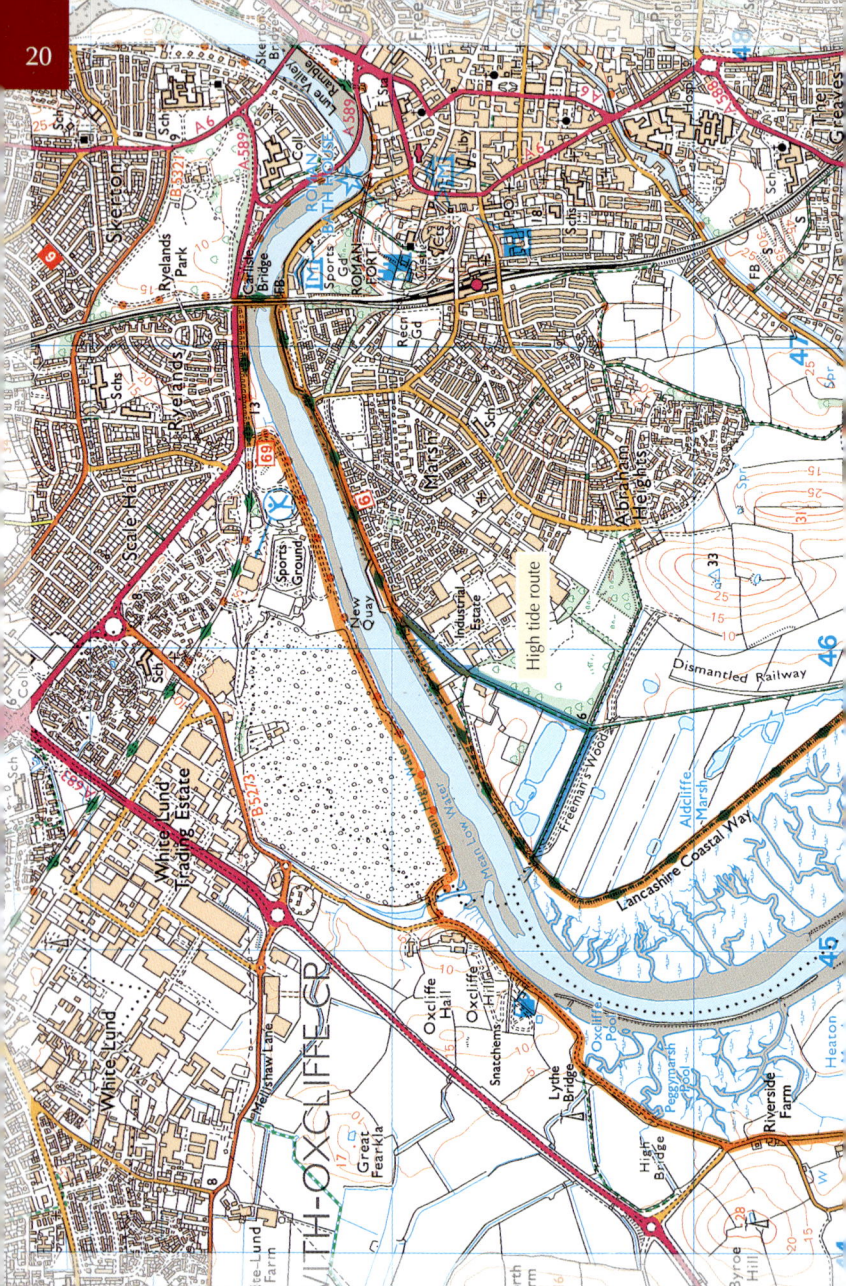

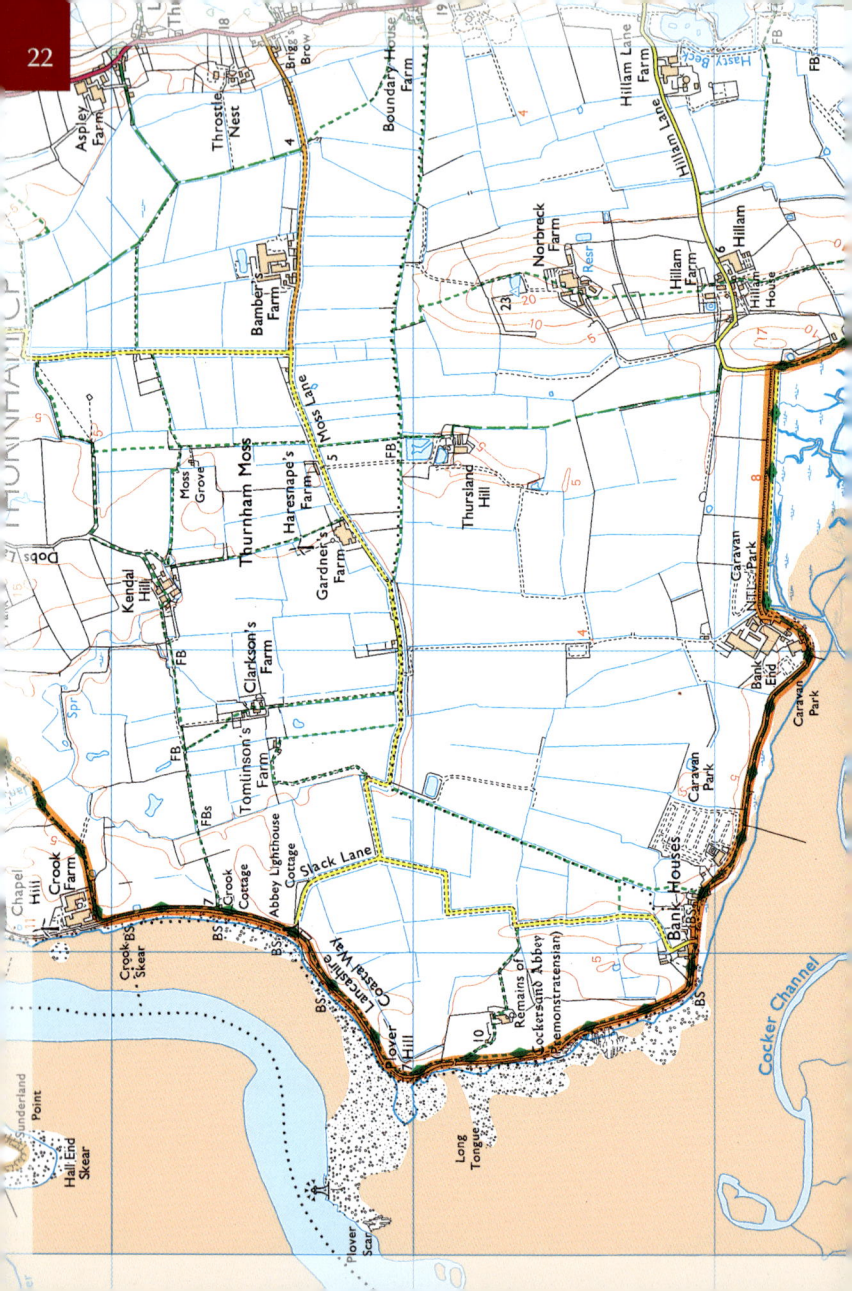

Use as main route from April to August
38
39
40
Worm Pool
Fluke Hall
BS
FB
Floodgate
Sandfield Cottage
Breck Bridge
Fluke Hall Lane
Fanny Bridge
Seafield
Ridge Farm
Old Ridge
Pilling Ridge
Bee House
Poultry Houses
Cocker's Dyke (Drain)
Carr House Farm
Muffy's Platt
Hotel
Ladies Hill
Sch
Wheel Lane
Townson Hill
Smithson's Farm
Hooles Farm
Smallwood Hey
Pasture House Farm
Bibby's Farm
Holme's Farm
Brookfield Farm
Ned's Lane
Abrahams Farm
Greenlands
Grange Cottages
Shaws
Carr Lane
Ox Close Lane
Bourbles Farm
The Crossing Cottage
Lamb's Lane
Adkinson's Wood
Baldwin's Wood
Shaw's Lane
Throstle's Nest Farm
Shawland's Farm
Lyndale Farm
A 588
Head Dyke
Squire's Gate Farm
Southlands Farm
Ashleigh Farm
New Lane Wood
Peartree Grove

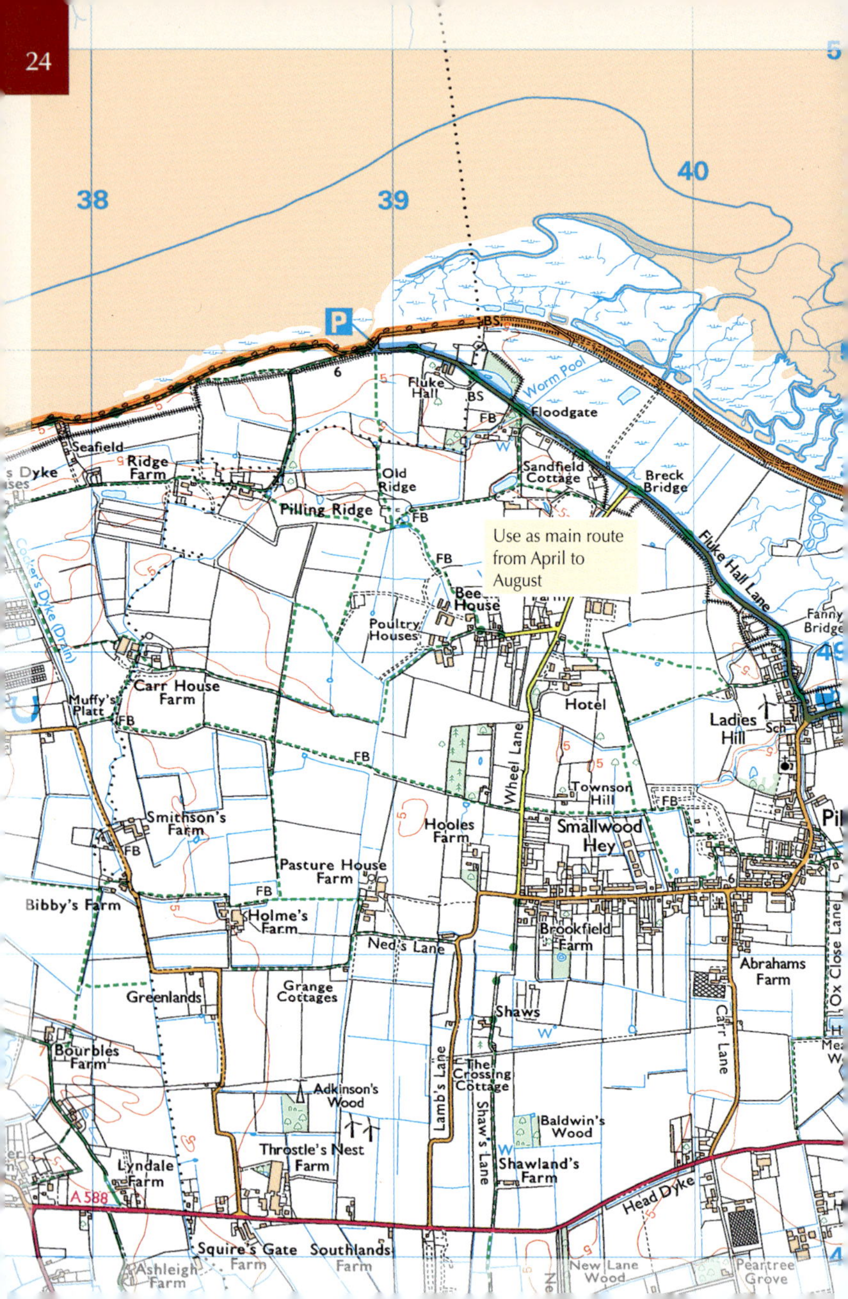

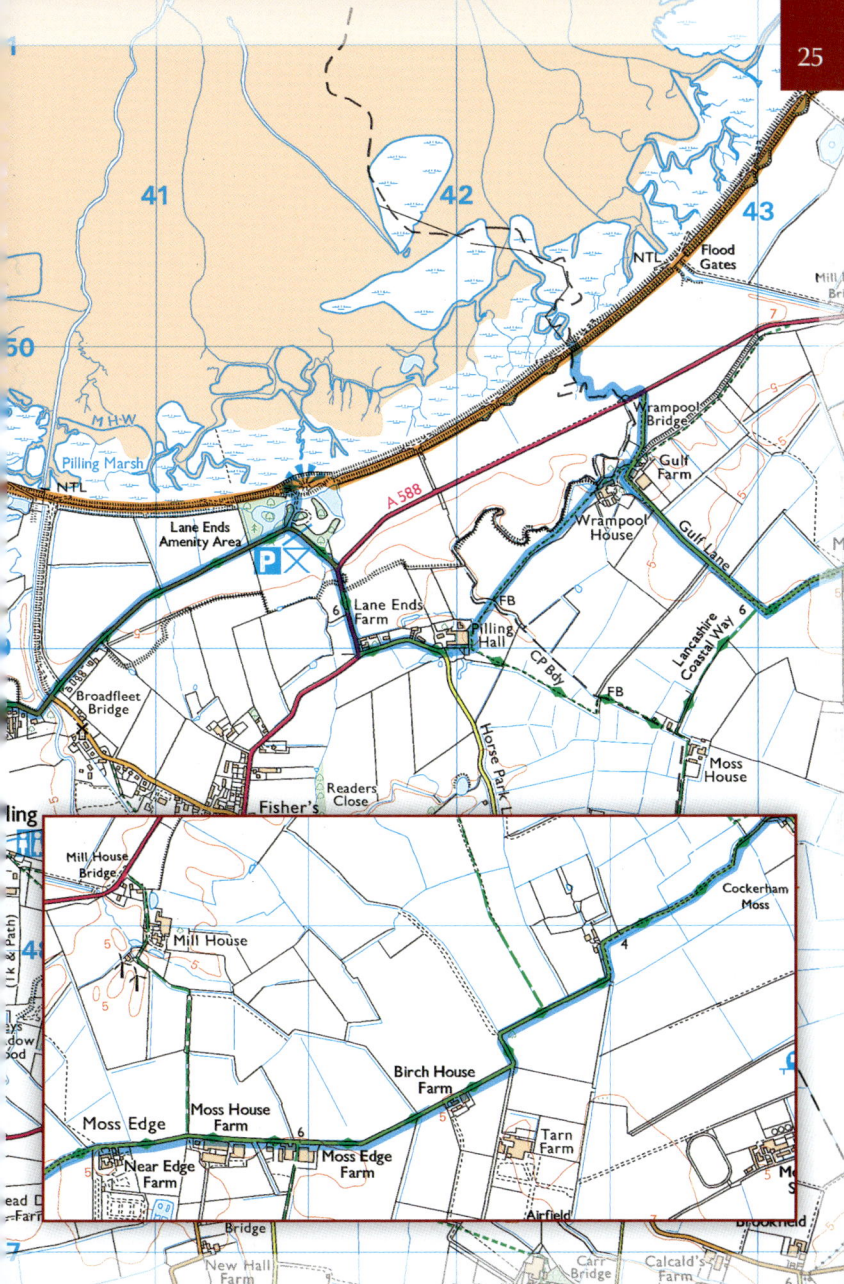

34

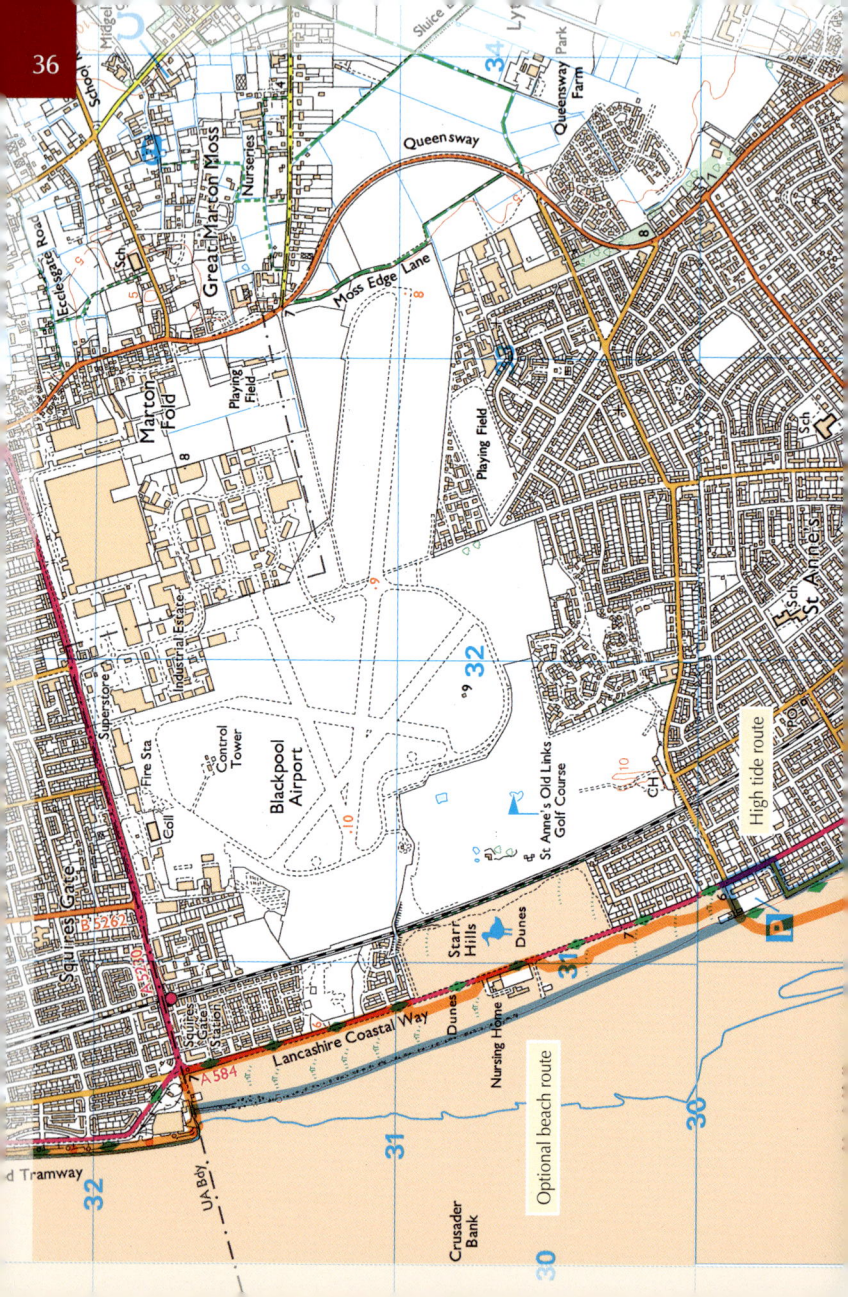

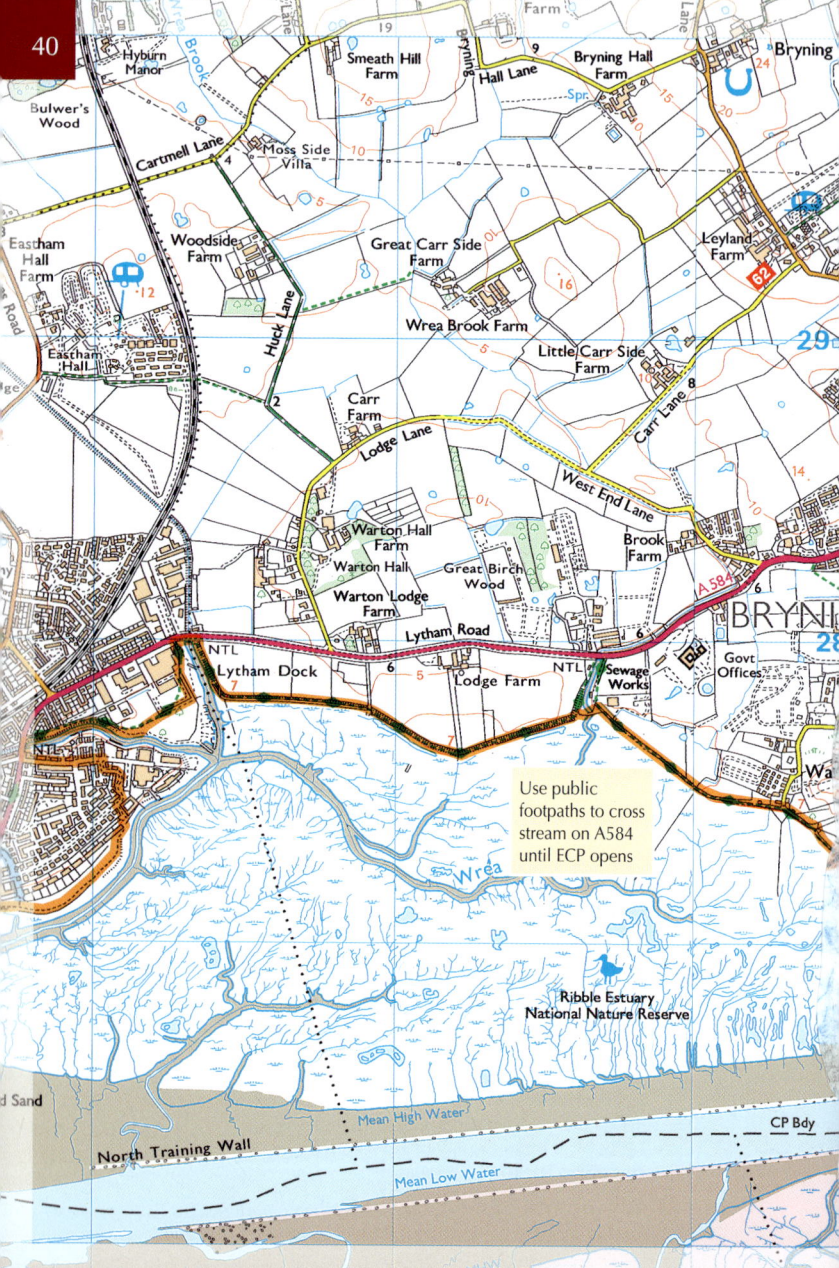

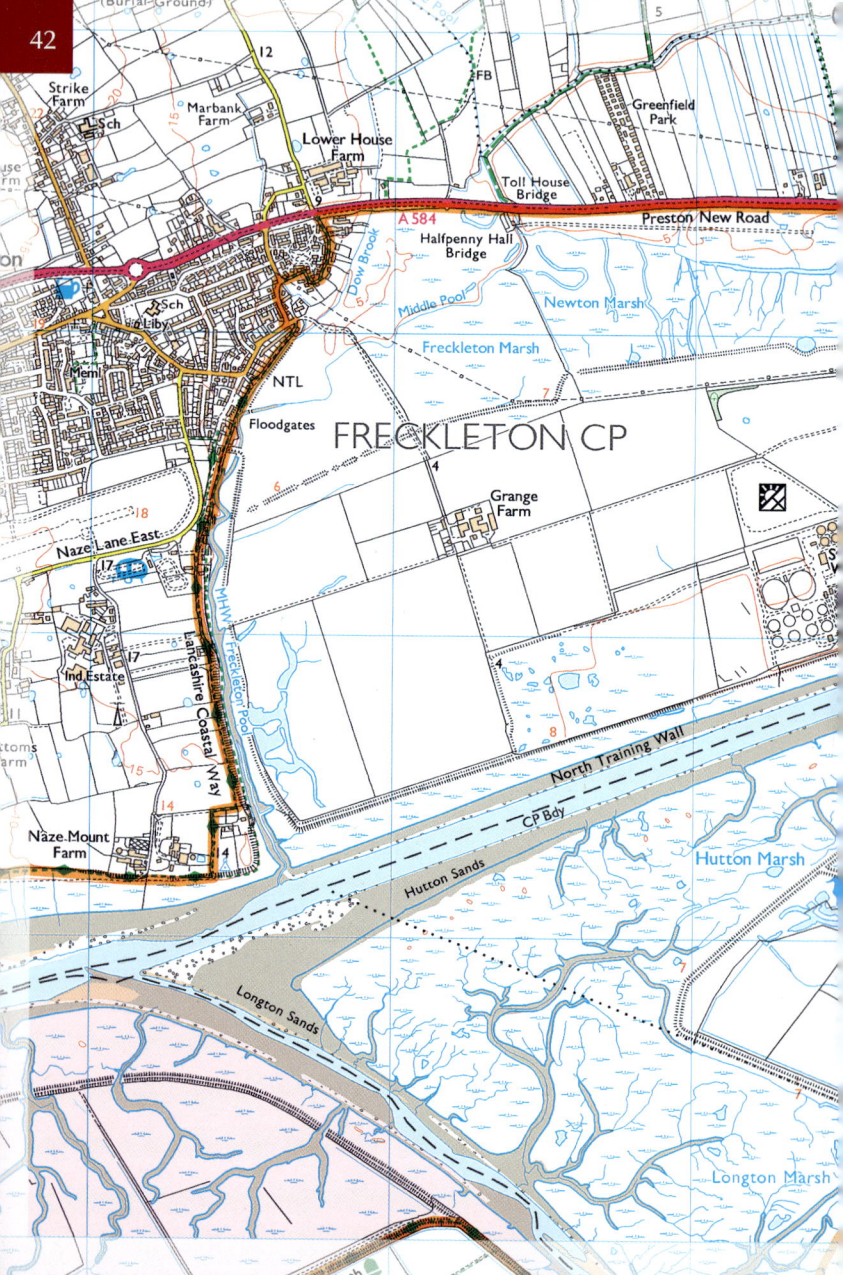

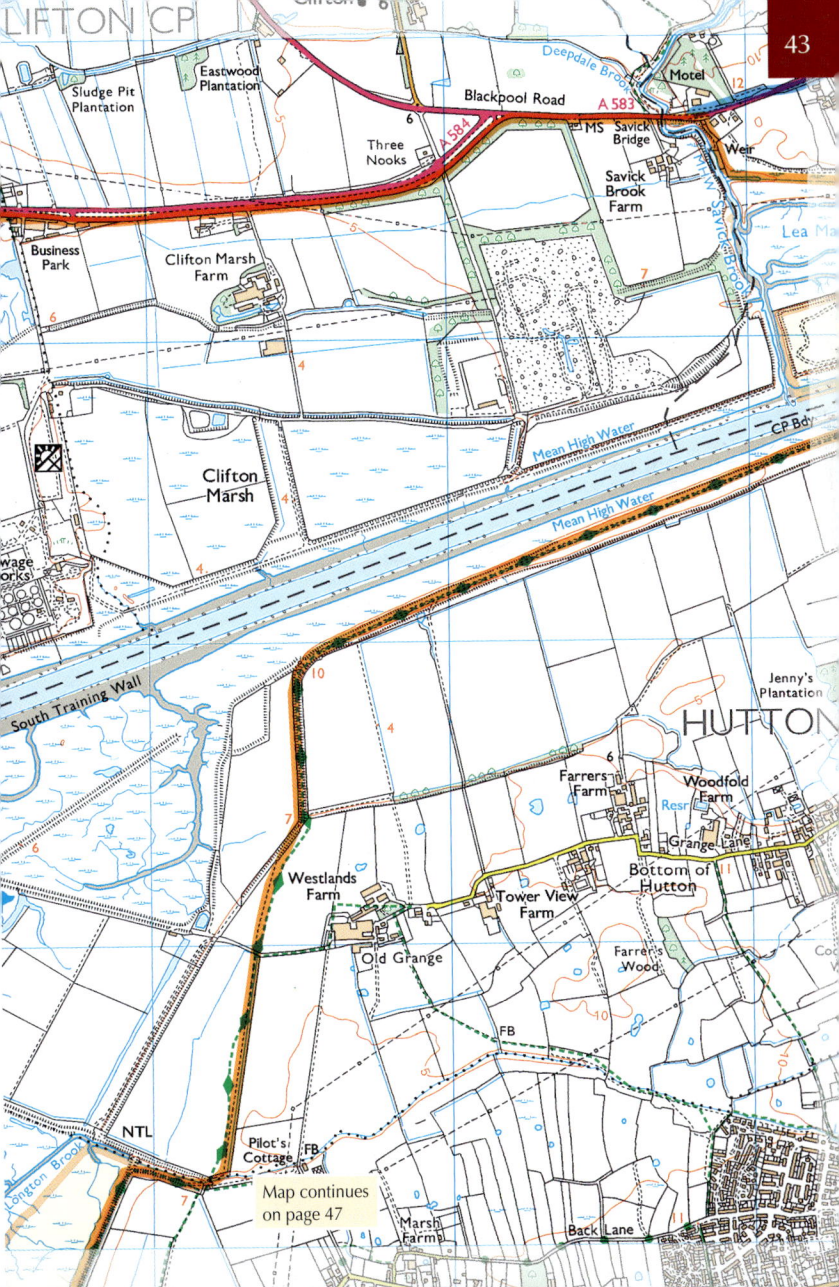

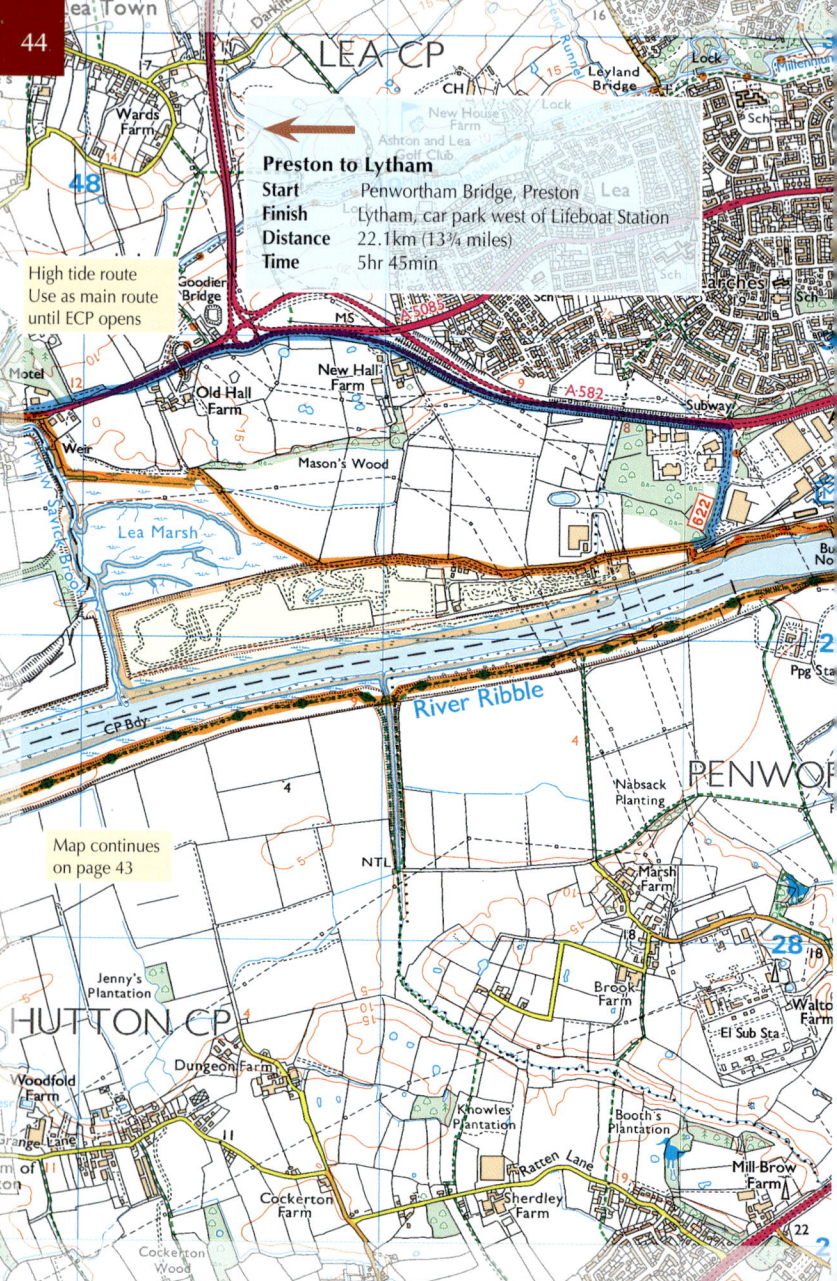

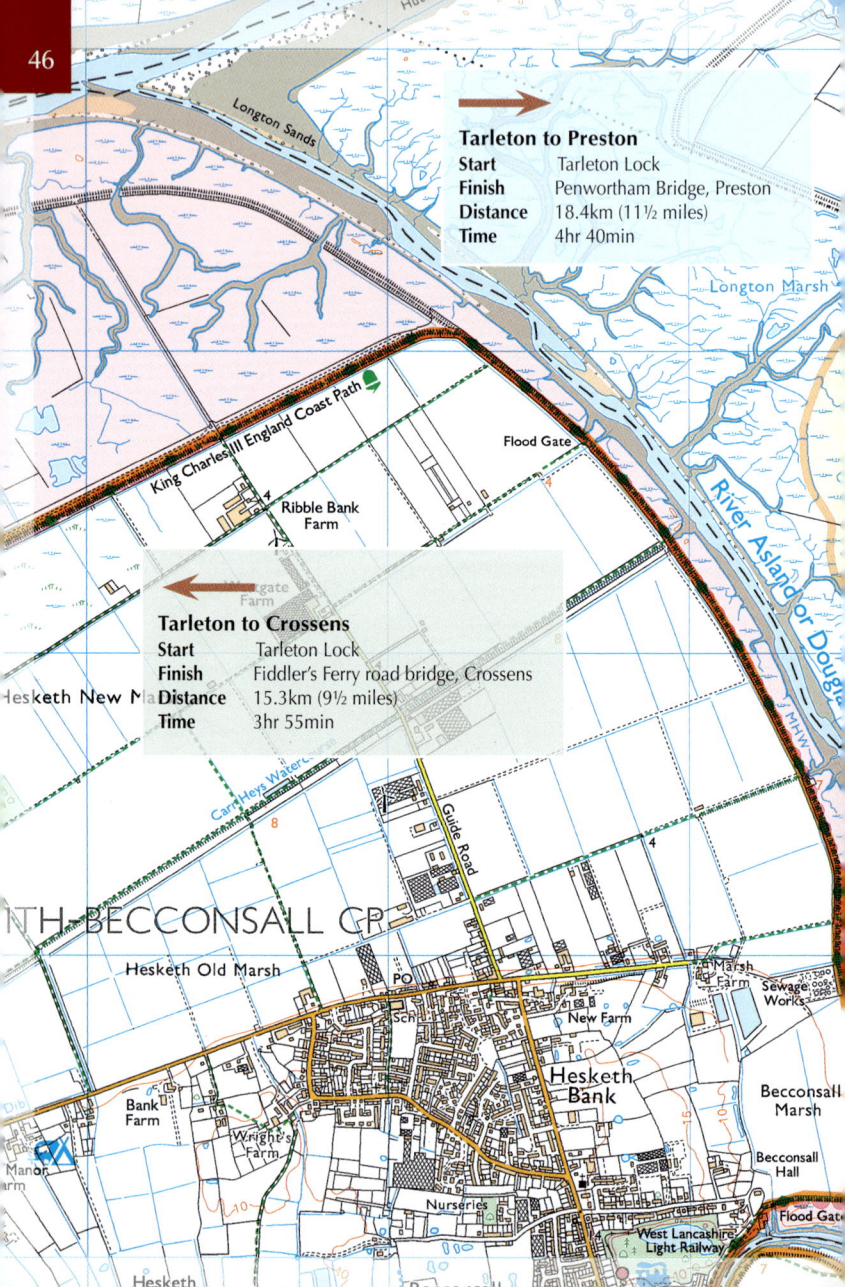

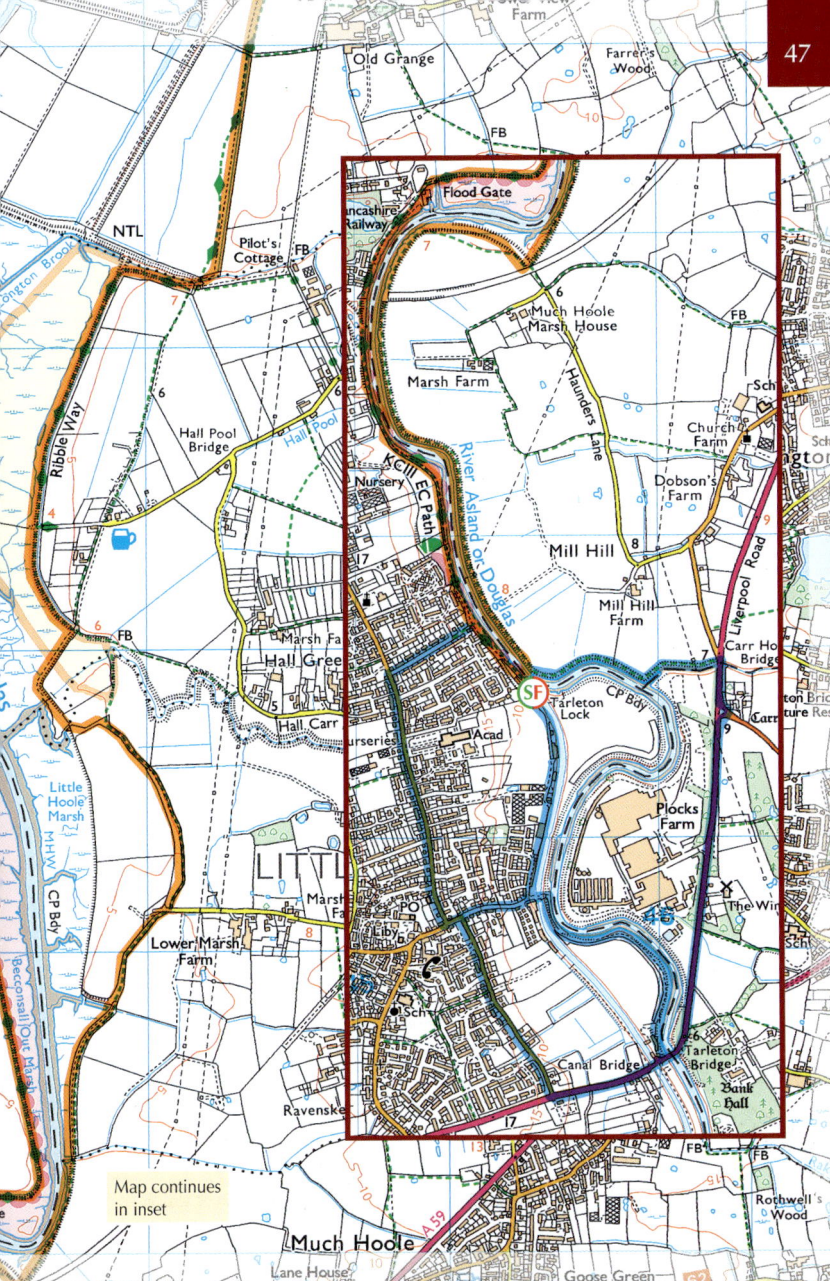

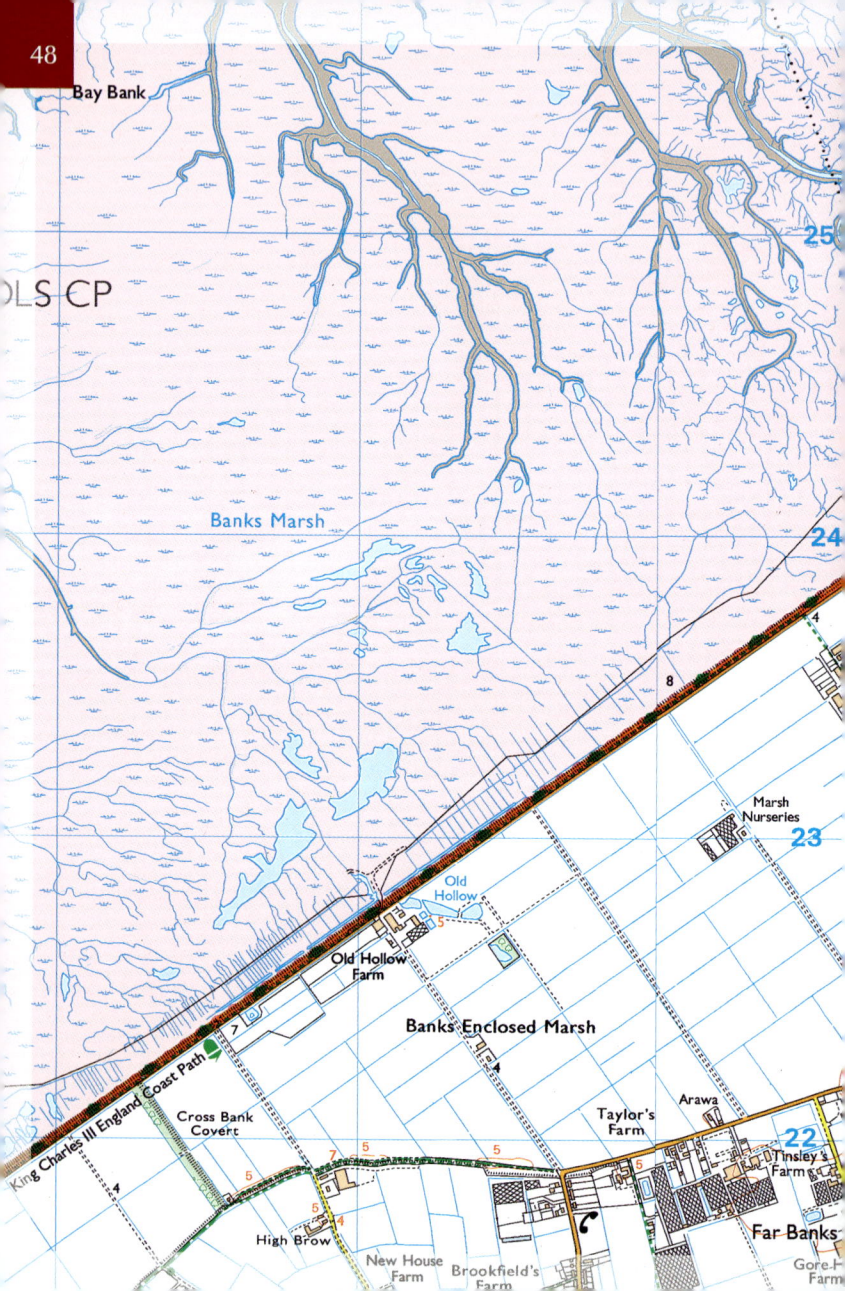

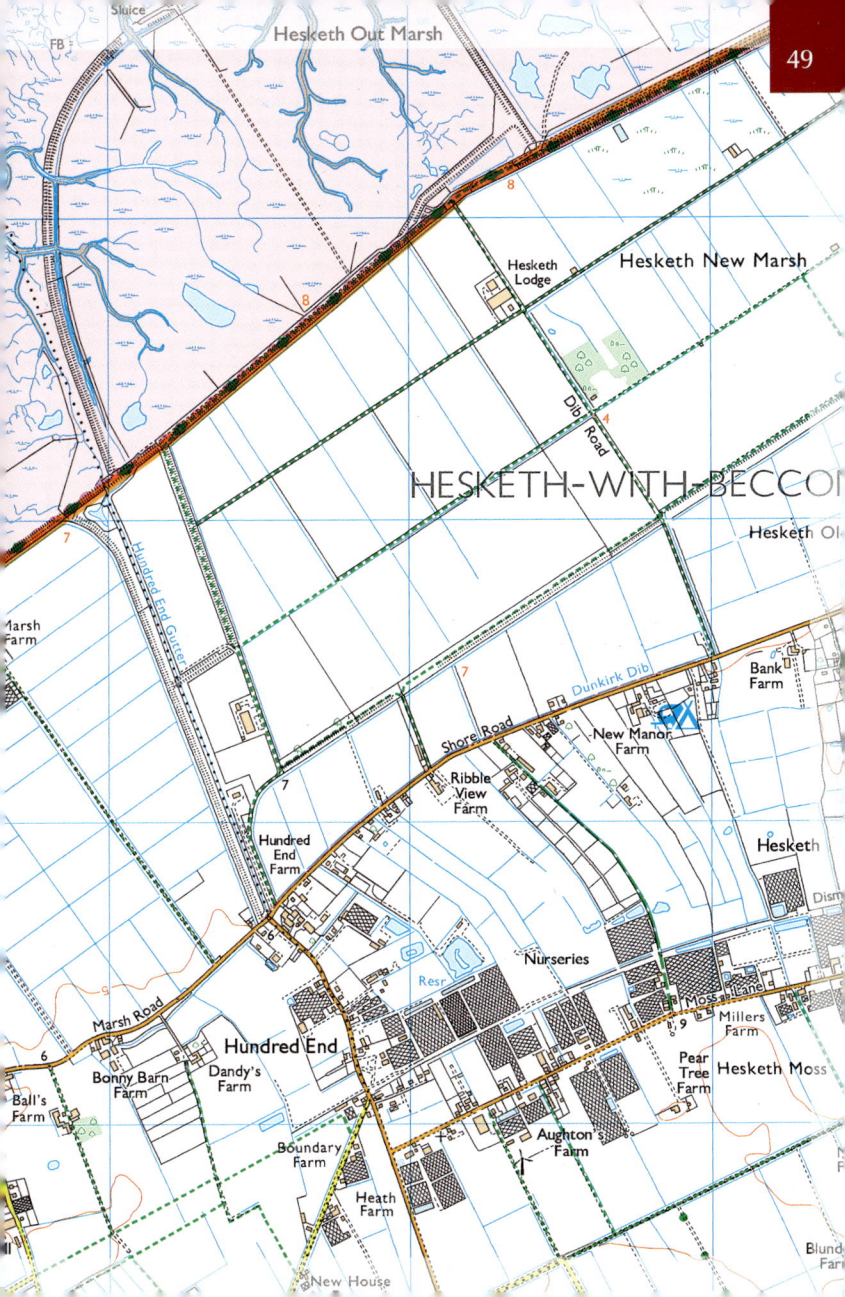

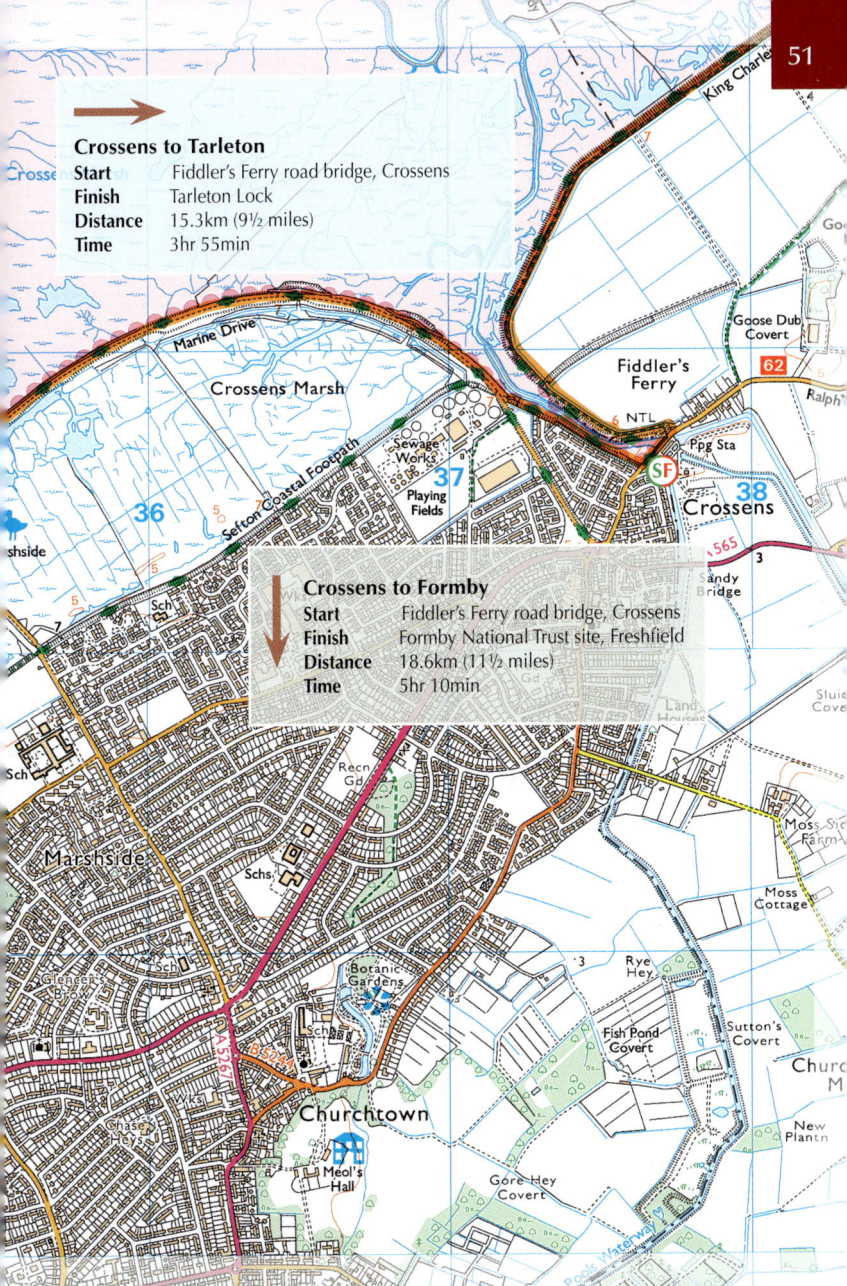

53

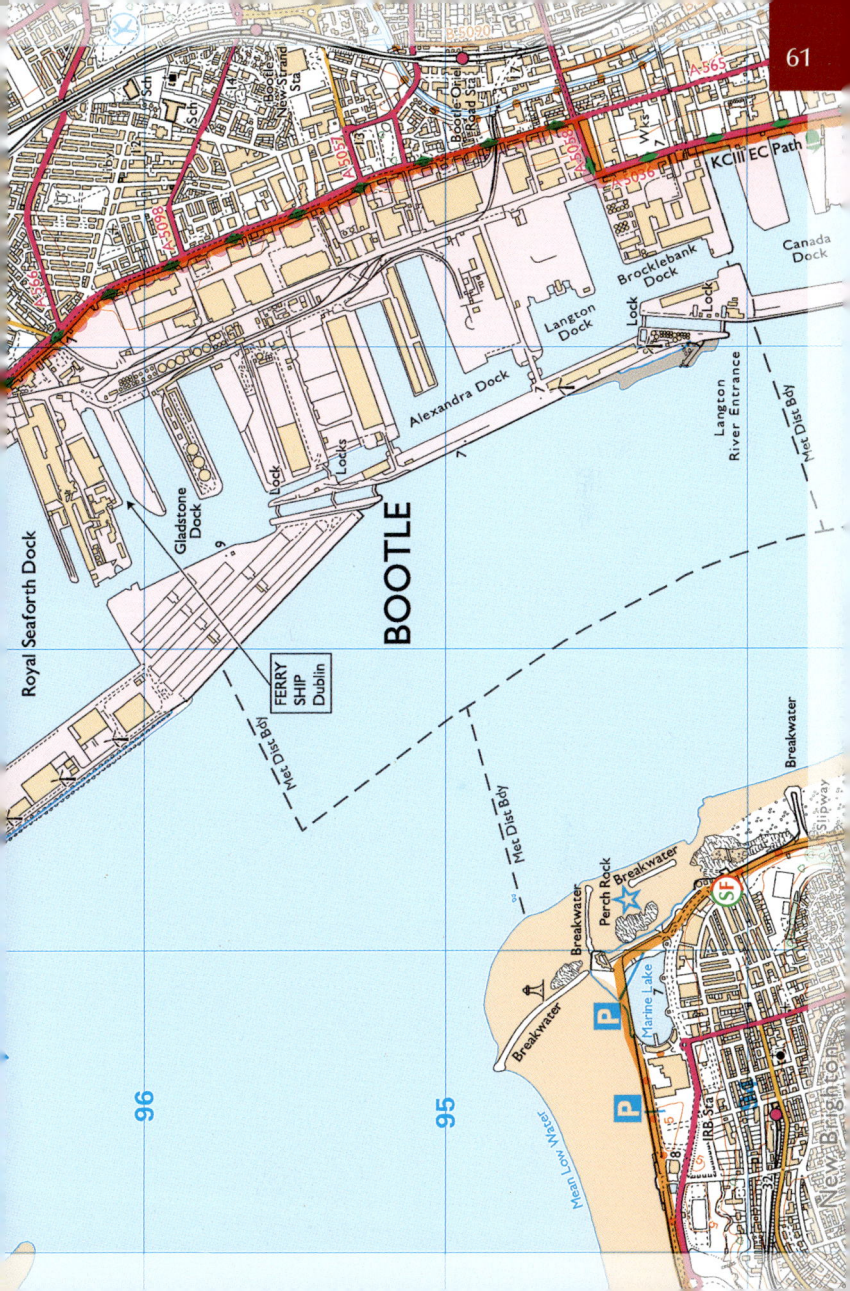

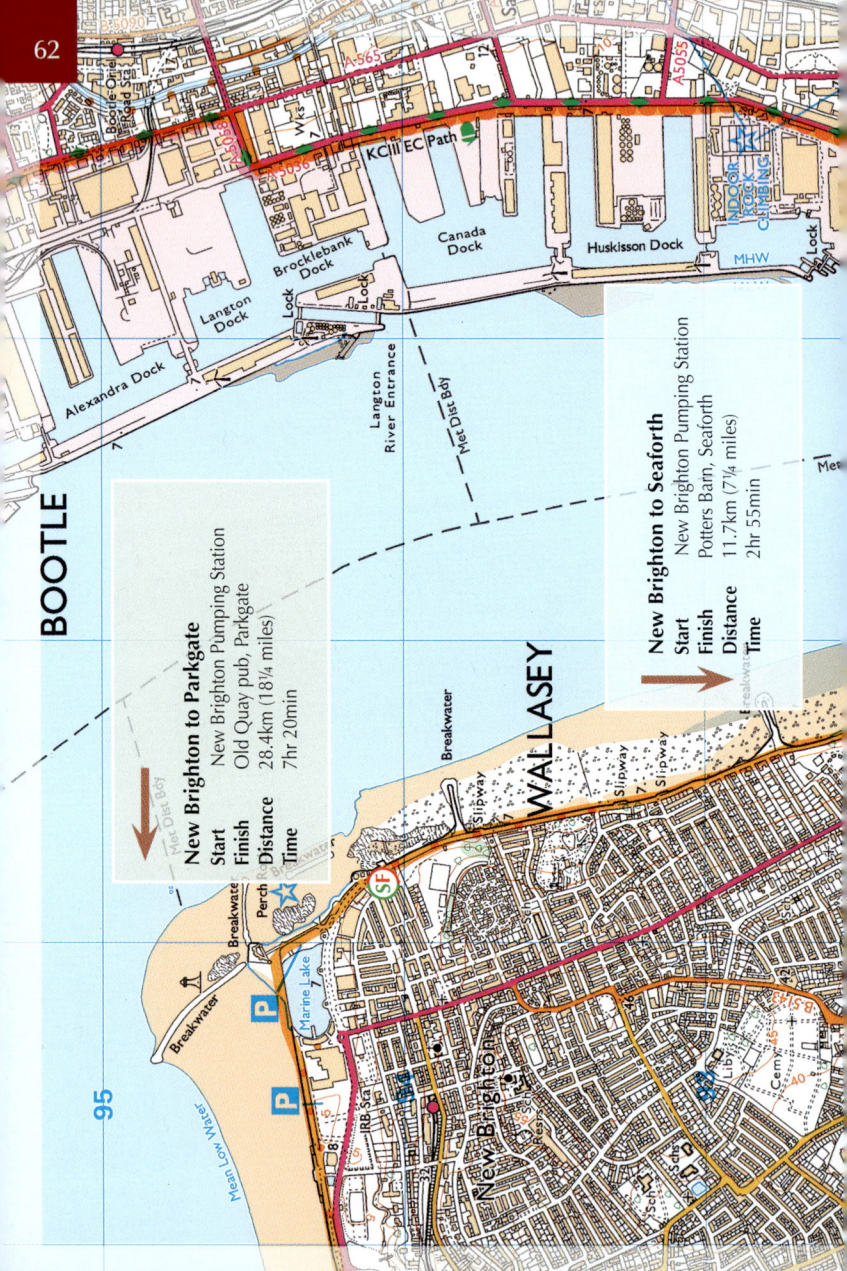

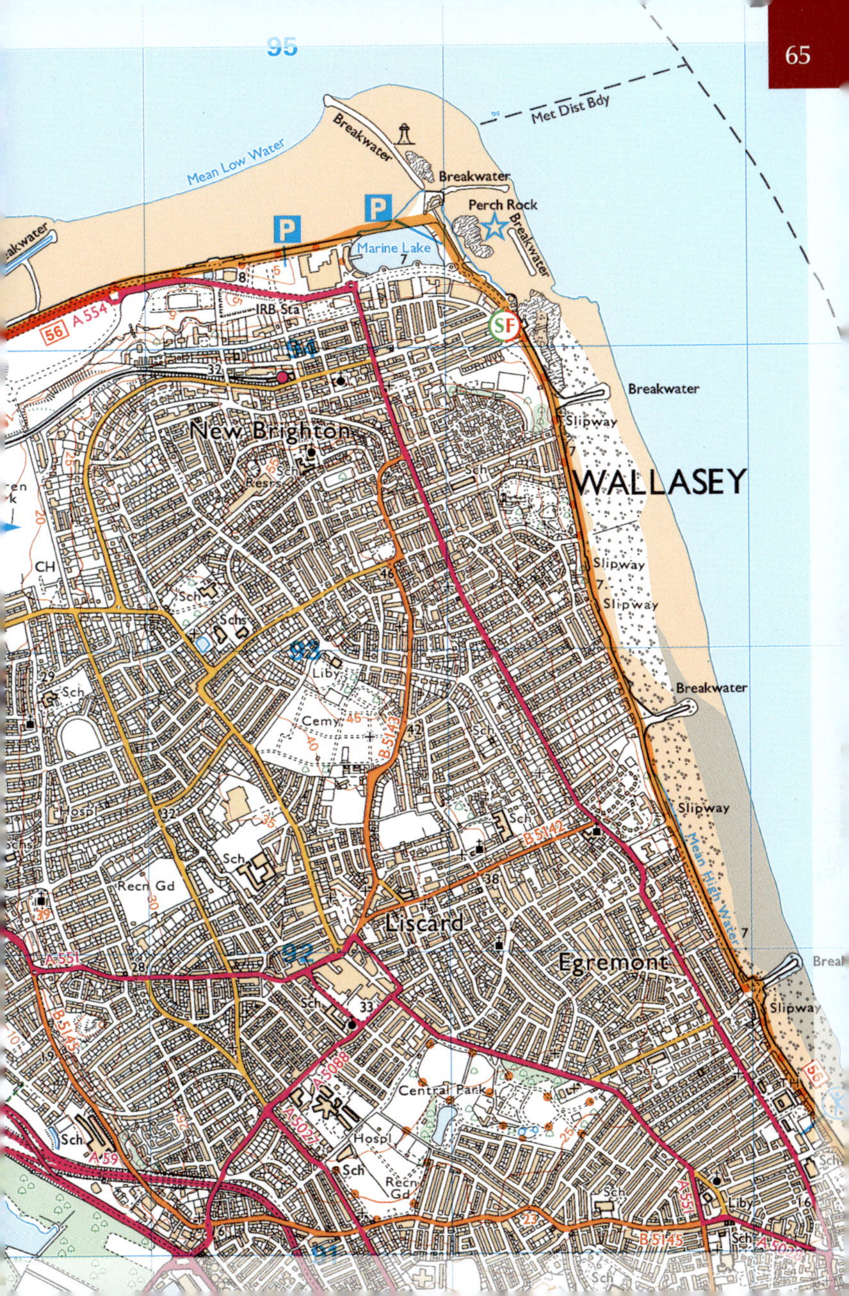

65

WALLASEY

New Brighton

Perch Rock

Breakwater

Marine Lake

IRB Sta

Liscard

Egremont

Central Park

Mean Low Water

Mean High Water

Met Dist Bdy

Slipway

A554

A551

A59

B5145

B5142

68

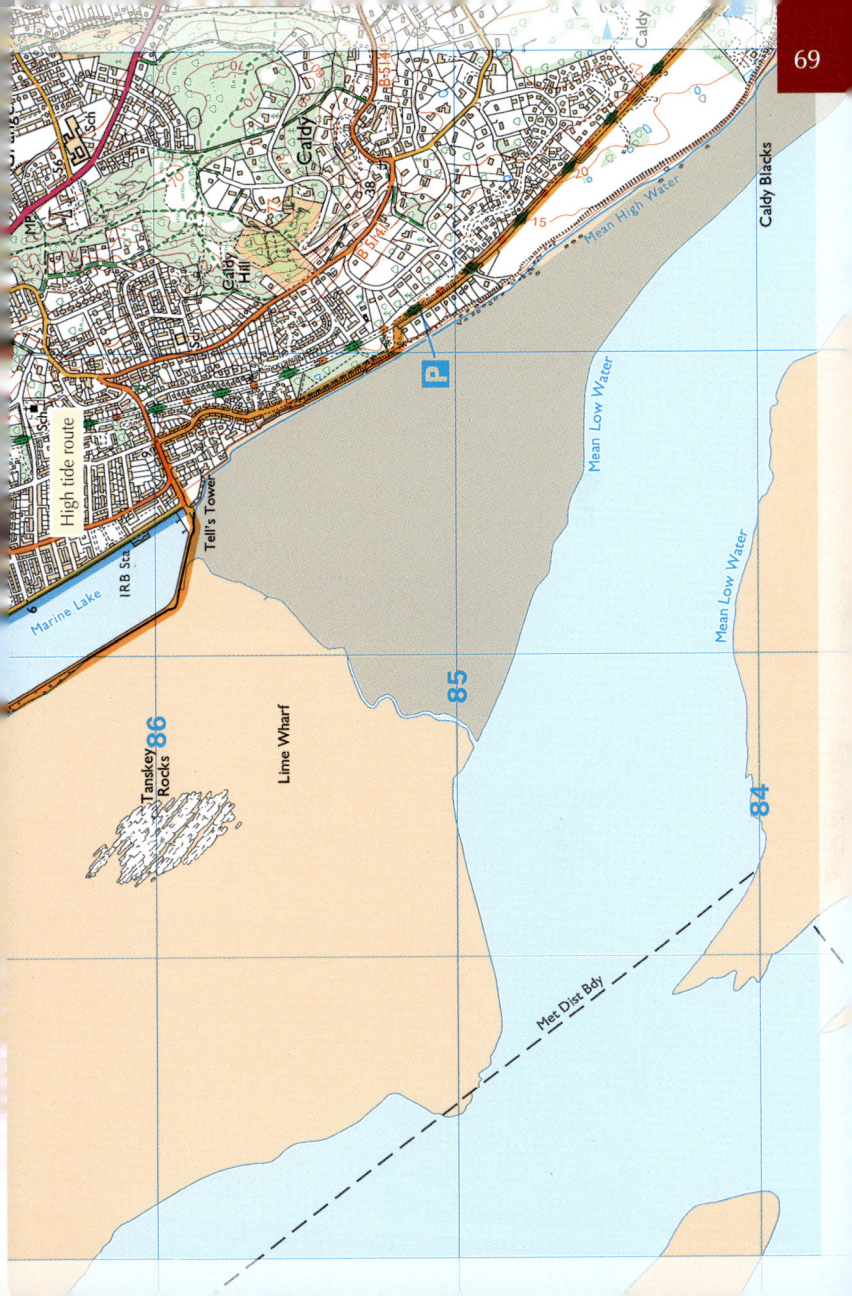

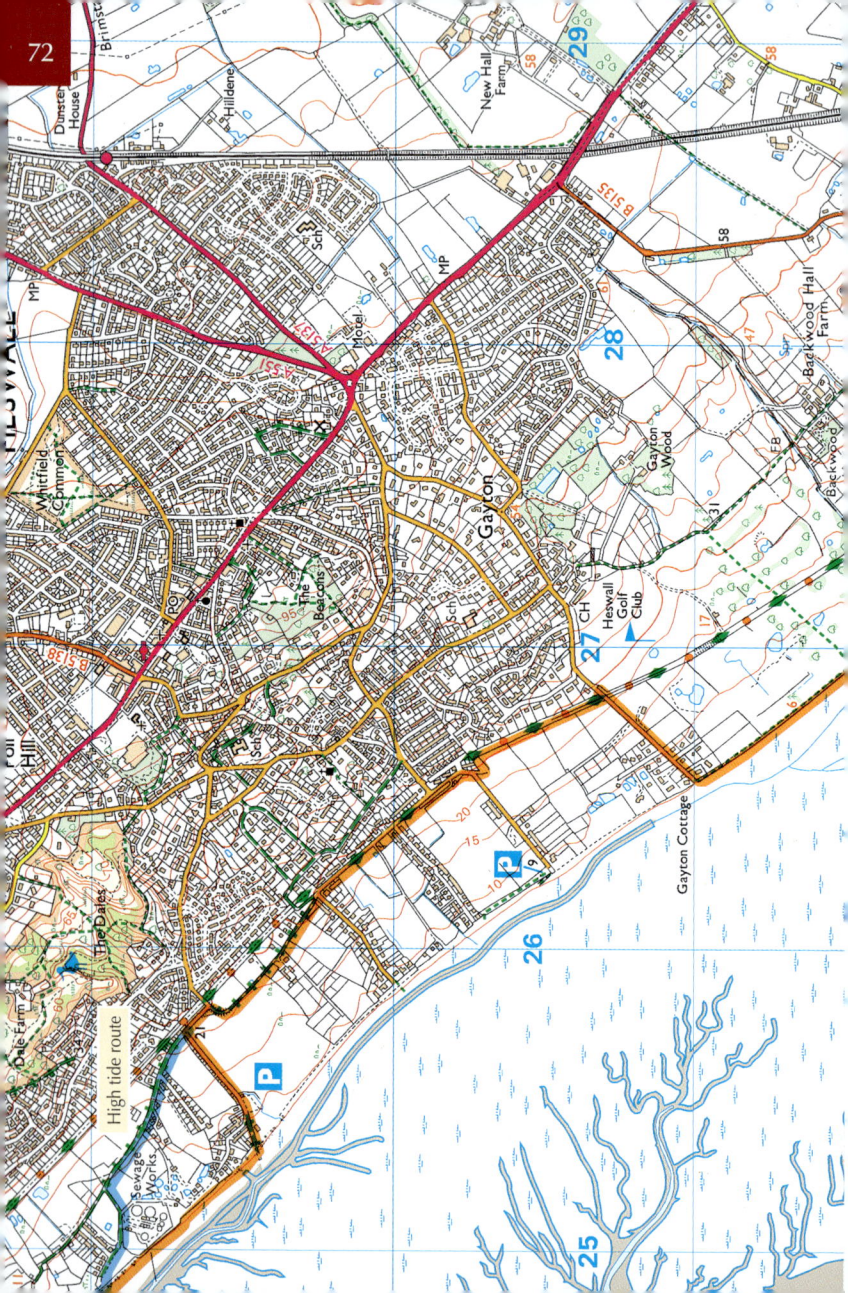

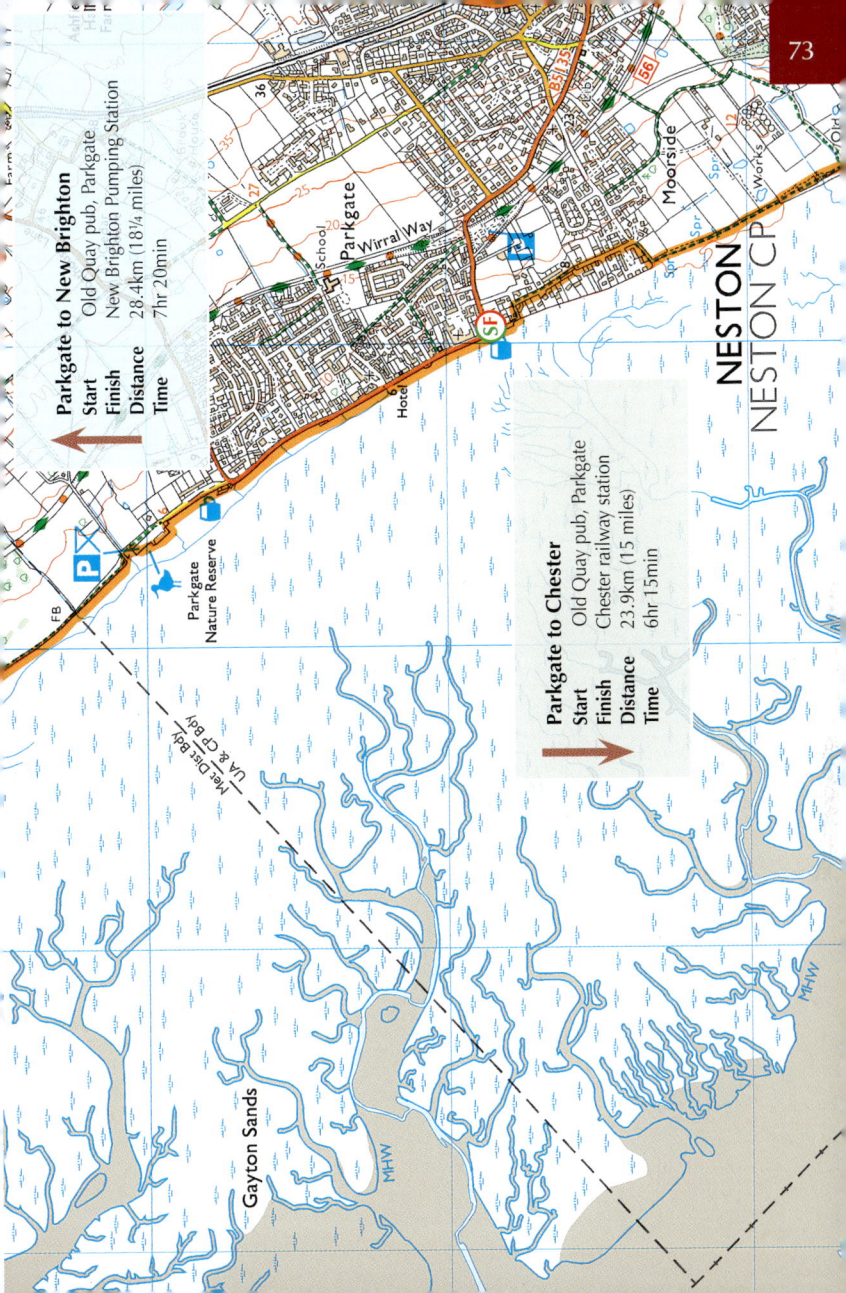

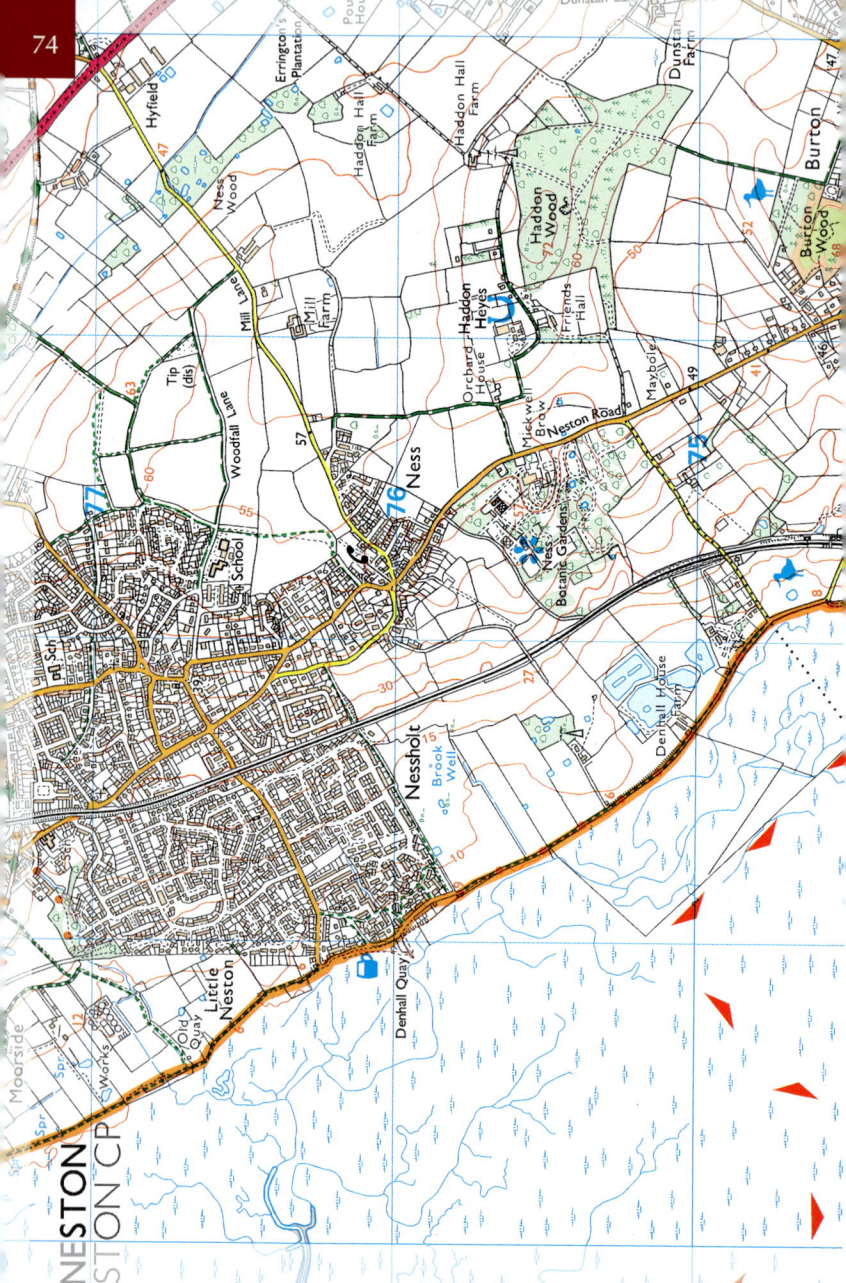

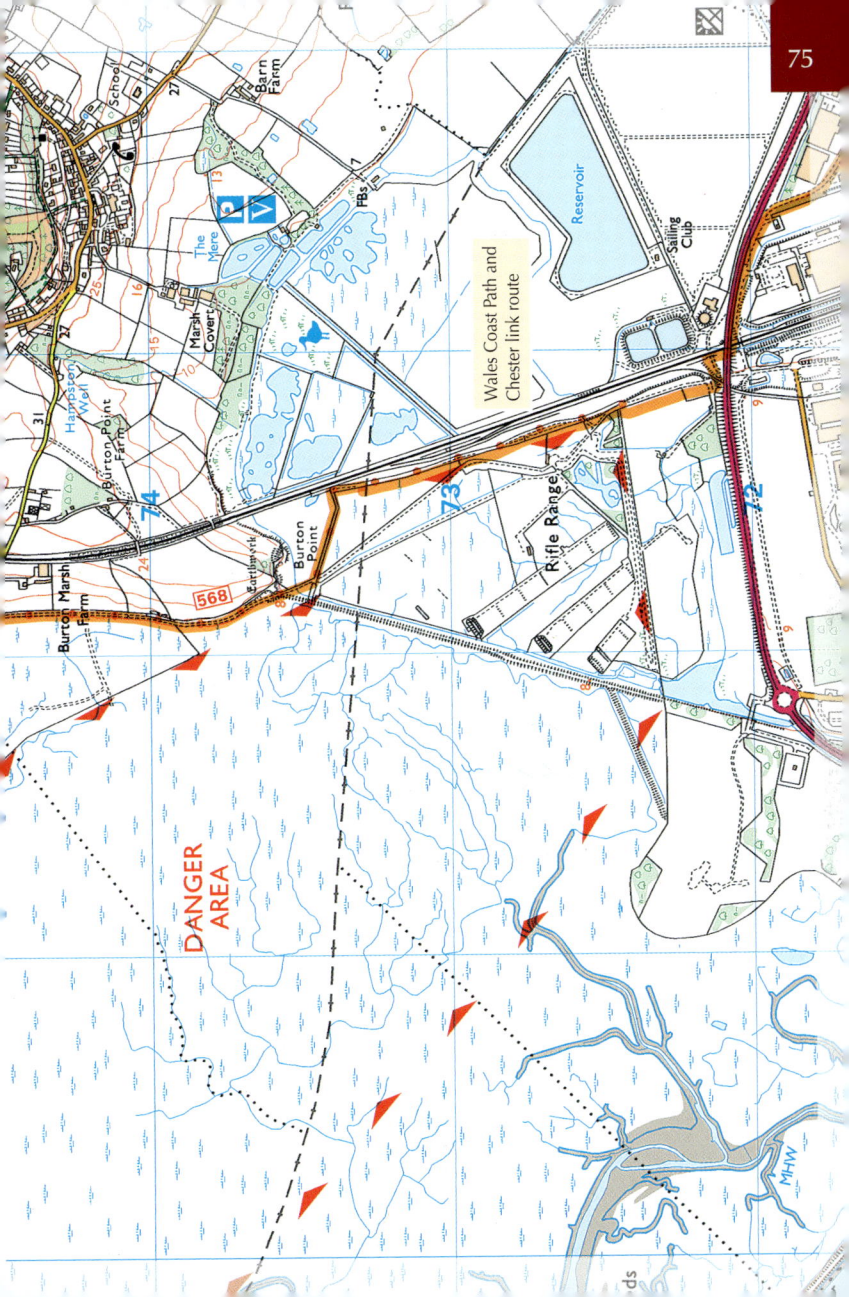

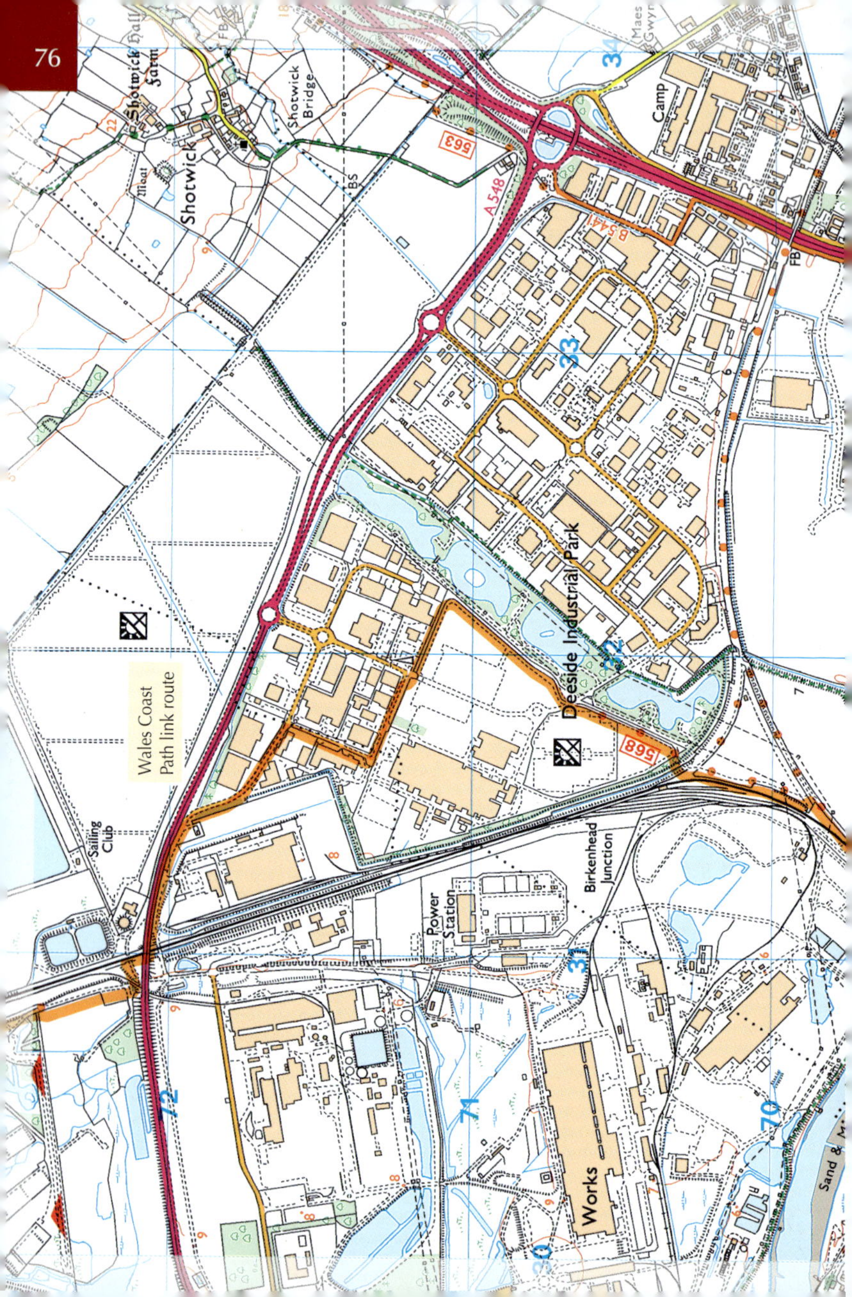

Shotwick
Shotwick Bridge
A548
Deeside Industrial Park
Wales Coast Path link route
Sailing Club
Power Station
Birkenhead Junction
Works

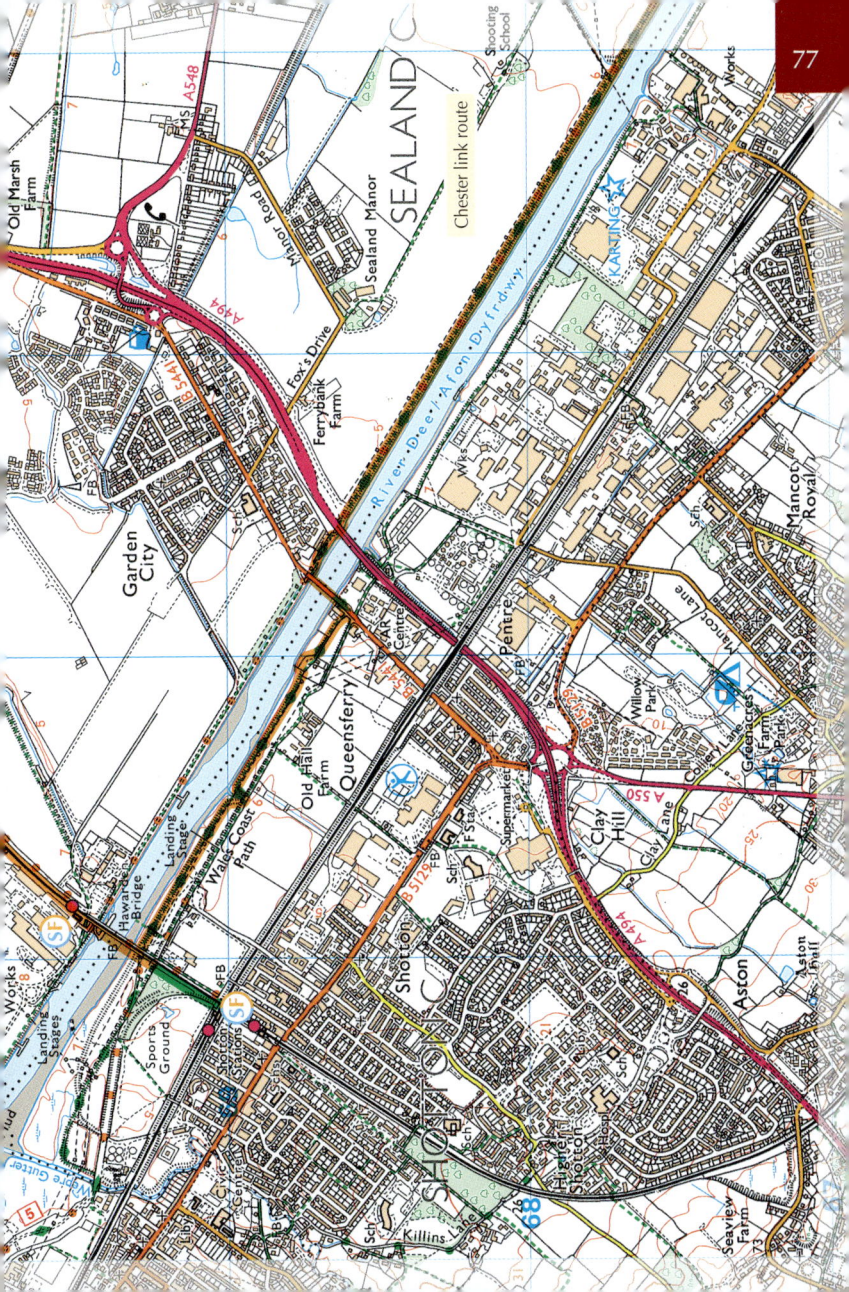

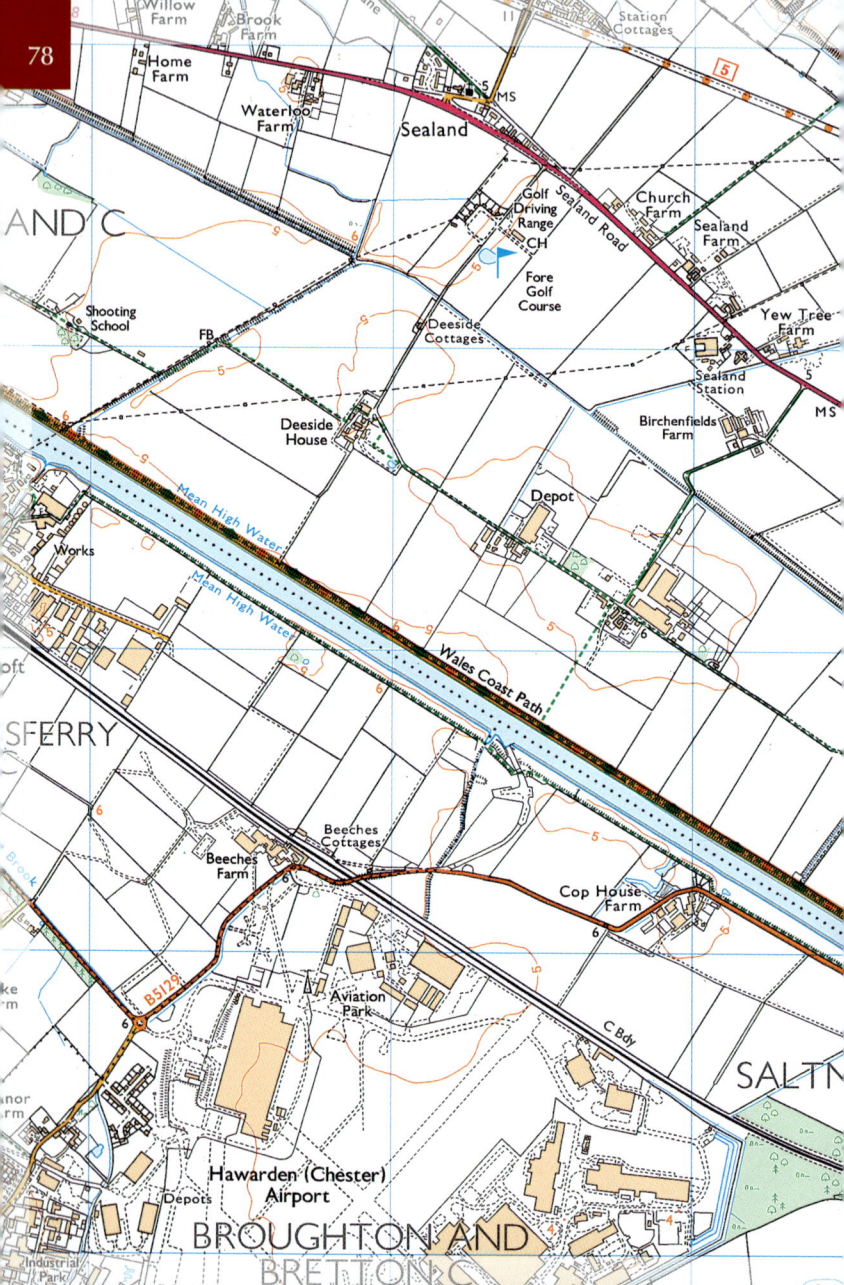

LEGEND OF SYMBOLS USED ON ORDNANCE SURVEY 1:25,000 (EXPLORER) MAPPING

ROADS AND PATHS — Not necessarily rights of way

Symbol	Description
M1 or A6(M)	Motorway
A 35	Dual carriageway
A30	Main road
B 3074	Secondary road
	Narrow road with passing places
	Road under construction
	Road generally more than 4 m wide
	Road generally less than 4 m wide
	Other road, drive or track, fenced and unfenced
>> →	Gradient: steeper than 20% (1 in 5); 14% (1 in 7) to 20% (1 in 5)
Ferry	Ferry; Ferry P – passenger only
	Path

Service Area (Motorway)
Service Area (Main road)
7 Junction Number
T1 Toll road junction

RAILWAYS

- Multiple track / Single track — standard gauge
- Narrow gauge or Light rapid transit system (LRTS) and station
- Road over; road under; level crossing
- Cutting; tunnel; embankment
- Station, open to passengers; siding

PUBLIC RIGHTS OF WAY

- - - - - - Footpath
— — — — Bridleway
+ + + + + Byway open to all traffic
-·-·-·-·- Restricted byway

The representation on this map of any other road, track or path is no evidence of the existence of a right of way

ARCHAEOLOGICAL AND HISTORICAL INFORMATION

Symbol	Description	Symbol	Description	Symbol	Description
⚔	Site of antiquity	VILLA	Roman	☆	Visible earthwork
⚔ 1066	Site of battle (with date)	Castle	Non-Roman		

Information provided by English Heritage for England and the Royal Commissions on the Ancient and Historical Monuments for Scotland and Wales

OTHER PUBLIC ACCESS

• • • • Other route with public access (not normally shown in urban areas)
The exact nature of the rights on these routes and the existence of any restrictions may be checked with the local highway authority. Alignments are based on the best information available

◆ ◆   🚶 National Trail / 🏴󠁧󠁢󠁳󠁣󠁴󠁿 Scotland's Great Trails   ◆ ◆ Recreational Route

◇ ◇   Alternative Route (England Coast Path only)

• • • Traffic-free cycle route

[1] National cycle network route number - traffic free   [1] National cycle network route number - on road

------------ Permissive footpath ⎫
                                 ⎬ Footpaths and bridleways along which landowners have permitted public use but which are not rights of way. The agreement may be withdrawn
− − − − − Permissive bridleway ⎭

Scotland

In Scotland, everyone has access rights in law* over most land and inland water, provided access is exercised responsibly. **This includes walking, cycling, horse-riding and water access, for recreational and educational purposes, and for crossing land or water.** Access rights do not apply to motorised activities, hunting, shooting or fishing, nor if your dog is not under proper control. The **Scottish Outdoor Access Code** is the reference point for responsible behaviour, and can be obtained at **www.outdooraccess-scotland.com** or by phoning your local Scottish Natural Heritage office.   *Land Reform (Scotland) Act 2003

National Trust for Scotland, always open / limited opening - observe local signs

Forestry Commission Land normally open - / Woodland Trust Land observe local signs

England, Scotland & Wales

Firing and test ranges in the area. Danger! Observe warning notices
Champs de tir et d'essai. Danger! Se conformer aux avertissements
Schieß und Erprobungsgelände. Gefahr! Warnschilder beachten
Visit **www.access.mod.uk** for information

ACCESS LAND

England & Wales

Access land portrayed on this map is intended as a guide to land normally available for access on foot, for example access land created under the Countryside and Rights of Way Act 2000, and land managed by National Trust, Forestry Commission and Woodland Trust. Some restrictions will apply; some land shown as access land may not have open access rights; always refer to local signage.

 Access land   Access information point   Access land in woodland area

Coastal margin

All land within the 'coastal margin' (where it already exists) is associated with the England Coast Path and is by default access land, but in some areas it contains land not subject to access rights – for example cropped land, buildings and their curtilage, gardens and land subject to local restrictions. Furthermore the coastal margin is often steep, unstable and not readily accessible. Please do not assume all the area shaded is accessible and take careful note of conditions and local signage on the ground.

For more information on coastal access check with the local authority or visit:
http://www.nationaltrail.co.uk/england-coast-path and **www.openaccess.naturalengland.org.uk**

ACCESS LAND (continued)

The depiction of rights of access does not imply or express any warranty as to its accuracy or completeness. Observe local signs and follow the Countryside Code.
Visit **www.naturalengland.org.uk/ourwork/enjoying/countrysidecode**

 Access permitted within managed controls, for example, local byelaws
Visit **www.access.mod.uk** for information

BOUNDARIES

— + — + — National

— · — · — County (England)

— — — — Unitary Authority (UA), Metropolitan District (Met Dist), London Borough (LB) or District
(Scotland & Wales are solely Unitary Authorities)

· · · · · · · · · Civil Parish (CP) (England) or Community (C) (Wales)

▬▬▬▬ National Park boundary

VEGETATION

Limits of vegetation are defined by positioning of symbols

Coniferous trees

Non-coniferous trees

Coppice

Orchard

Scrub

Bracken, heath or rough grassland

Marsh, reeds or saltings

HEIGHTS AND NATURAL FEATURES

52 · Ground survey height
284 · Air survey height

Surface heights are to the nearest metre above mean sea level. Where two heights are shown, the first height is to the base of the triangulation pillar and the second (in brackets) to the highest natural point of the hill

Vertical face/cliff

Loose rock | Boulders | Outcrop | Scree

Contours are at 5 or 10 metre vertical intervals

Water

Mud

Sand; sand and shingle

SELECTED TOURIST AND LEISURE INFORMATION

 Building of historic interest

 Cadw

 Heritage centre

 Camp site

 Caravan site

Camping and caravan site

 Nature reserve

 National Trust

 Other tourist feature

Parking

Park and ride, all year

 Park and ride, seasonal

SELECTED TOURIST AND LEISURE INFORMATION (continued)

Symbol	Description	Symbol	Description
	Castle / fort		Picnic site
	Cathedral / Abbey		Preserved railway
	Craft centre	PC	Public Convenience
	Country park		Public house/s
	Cycle trail		Recreation / leisure / sports centre
	Mountain bike trail		Roman site (Hadrian's Wall only)
	Cycle hire		Slipway
	English Heritage		Telephone, emergency
	Fishing		Telephone, public
	Forestry Commission Visitor centre		Telephone, roadside assistance
	Garden / arboretum		Theme / pleasure park
	Golf course or links		Viewpoint
	Historic Scotland	V	Visitor centre
	Information centre, all year		Walks / trails
	Information centre, seasonal		World Heritage site / area
	Horse riding		Water activites
	Museum		Boat trips
	National Park Visitor Centre (park logo) e.g. Yorkshire Dales		Boat hire

(For complete legend and symbols, see any OS Explorer map).

NOTES

WALKING THE KING CHARLES III ENGLAND COAST PATH: NORTH WEST

This map booklet accompanies Ange Harker's guidebook to walking the King Charles III England Coast Path, from Gretna to Chester. The guidebook features 1:50,000 OS mapping alongside detailed step-by-step route description and lots of planning and other information about local culture, wildlife and the protected coastline.

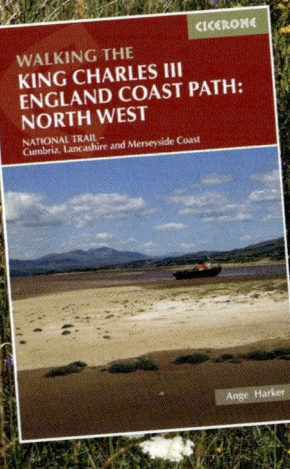

A range of nectar-rich summer flowers bring colour to the Raven Meols dune grasslands (Stage 25)

CICERONE

Trust Cicerone to guide your next adventure, wherever it may be around the world...

Discover guides for hiking, mountain walking, backpacking, trekking, trail running, cycling and mountain biking, ski touring, climbing and scrambling in Britain, Europe and worldwide.

Connect with Cicerone online and find inspiration.

- buy books and ebooks
- articles, advice and trip reports
- GPX files and updates
- regular newsletter

cicerone.co.uk